DECLARATIONS OF THE
HEART

Raymond L. Gray
(Buddy)

Copyright © 2008
Declarations of the Heart
Raymond L. Gray
All rights reserved

Library of Congress Control Number 2008929653
ISBN 978-0-9715830-1-6

Printed in the United States
By: Morris Publishing
          3212 East Highway 30
          Kearney, NE 68847
          1-800-650-7888

INTRODUCTION

This is a collection of my poetry written over a half-century of living. May they bring you the joy that I knew when writing them. Happy reading!

DEDICATION

My three sons and their families, Raymond A. Gray, David G. Gray and Christopher L. Gray; my constant and loving companion and partner, Linda Mills, for her strength and support; my church family – The Portage First United Methodist Church, awesome disciples of Our Lord.

TABLE OF CONTENTS

SECTION ONE:
FAMILY

WINDOW OF DREAMS

I peered through the window of childhood memories
Seeking the wonders that once were there,
But the magic of imagination was missing
And I wondered if time is fair.

> Where have they all gone?
> Those magical, wondrous scenes
> That captured for a moment your being
> A part of a little child's dream.

> > Listen to the children around you
> > As through the window you peek.
> > The magic and wonder is in them
> > They are the memory you seek.

A SPECIAL LOVE

Babies are created in Heaven,
Their mothers chosen with care,
Then placed beneath her heart for awhile
As each other's love they share.

The nursery in Heaven was crowded
And a new life needing love
Was given to a special mother
By our dear Lord above.

Angels in Heaven rejoice
As a baby girl is placed
Beneath a loving heart
Blessed by God's Holy Grace.

Their needs will always be special.
Mother and Daughter are one.
As they cherish one another
Our Heavenly Father's will is done.

FIVE YEARS OLD

She was just a little girl, barely five
With a tiny turned-up nose
Wearing makeup on her face
And powder on her clothes.

She stood as tall
As a little girl could be
And tilted her head
To look up at me.

Her eyes were sparkling
With a little girl smile
Pretending to be grown-up
For just a while.

I held out my arms
With a tear in my eye
And she snuggled up close
With a little girl's sigh

Catching the scent of bubble gum
And the fragrance of Estee Lauder,
I smiled as I hugged this little girl
My make-believe grown-up daughter.

A CHILD'S HEART

The heart of a child is fragile
And will break if not handled with care.
Hold them close in your arms while they're learning
For they need to know you are there.

The words "I love you" broken by sobs
From a child who thinks he's done wrong
Tears at the heart of being a parent
And you need God's strength to be strong.

The heart of a child mends quickly
When the magic of love is applied.
Their world is filled with laughter
And they forget the times they cried.

In all our hearts there lives that child
That could not always be
A little boy or a little girl
In a world of fantasy.

MOM

I want your arms around me
To feel again the joy,
I knew so long ago
When I was but a boy.

You are the fairest of the fair,
A mother supreme,
And you will always be
My special beauty queen.

I thank you for the loving care
That brightened every day
And Mom, I'll always love you
As that boy did yesterday.

LIFE'S PERFECT MELODY

Children are not "throw-away" love.
There is no such a thing
They are the notes in life's song
That all God's angels sing.

Children are God's composition
Created to bring joy...
A happy tune of living
That comes as girl or boy.

Gather them in your arms
And sing their joyous song.
Repeat the chorus of love.
Make it a "sing-along".

Children are always searching
For beautiful harmony.
The sound is one of love...
Life's perfect melody.

MOTHER

God created woman
And the world was given
It's most beautiful flower.
She brought with her
Love and new life
And man was made whole
By Our Lord's creation.
Chosen by Our Lord
As the receptacle of life,
She is truly God's Angel
Delivering each of us
Into the world with eternal love.
We honor her with many titles
None of which have more meaning
Than "MOTHER".
She is the beginning
Of our "World Without End".

THE MOST BEAUTIFUL FLOWER

A flower chosen from a field of blossoms
Becomes more beautiful when blooming alone,
Sharing with you its fragrance
So sweet and true.

A woman with the inward strength and beauty
Given by our Lord,
Is more beautiful by far
Than His most exquisite flower.
She has a special love to share with someone,
So they need never be alone,
Forever giving happiness.

A man must hold the blossom given him
Close to his heart and with loving care,
They will become as one.
Their love will be nurtured by God
And their happiness bring forth a gift of life.

The most beautiful flower shall be called
          Mother
Her partner in living
          Father
And their gift of life
          Child
Together they are
          Family

MY MOTHER

If I could only once more be
A little one at my mother's knee,
I'd give most anything.

The loving comfort of her arms
Always kept me safe from harm,
She was my everything.

The sleepless nights when I was ill
And the early-morning hours still,
She was there.

The games and laughter we both shared
Were life's pure joy with no love spared,
She made me happy.

She tried to teach me right from wrong
And when needed, to be strong,
She knew those things.

And then one day when I was grown
And thought that I could live alone,
I had her love.

I can't go back, for she's not there
But I remember my mother's care.
I'm still her little one.

MOTHER'S LOVE

The little child in us
Is always there,
Remembering Mom's touch
And her loving care.

The comfort of her lap,
And the warmth of her arms.
A haven of rest
Safe from harm.

Happy Mother's Day, Mom
From children grown
Giving your love
To kids of their own.

How grateful we are
To have you here
And share in the love
Of a Mom so dear.

TO MY MOTHER – FROM ROSEMARY

Mothers become more precious
With every passing year…
Always there with love
To blot away each tear.

God gave me His love
And you carried me through
The portals of life,
As He prepared you to do.

You are a special picture
I carry in my heart…
Of love and understanding
From which I'll never part.

MAMA

How many times a day do I call you
And you are always there?
No matter your busy schedule
You find time to share.

I am only a kid
And I belong to you
You fill my life with love
And happy days too.

Everything I am,
I am because of you.
I need you to love me
In everything I do.

I have no secrets
I need to share.
You make my life a joy
Because every day you care.

Your loving son...

THANK YOU, MOM

A cool thin hand with small blue veins etched by time
clasped mine and at our touch, a special love
warmed my heart.

As I held this fragile, beautiful lady close in my arms,
time quickly reversed itself...and I was the one being
held on my first day of life.

Through my tears, all that I could see was yesterday,
and I lovingly whispered, "Thank you, Mom".

MOTHER'S DAY

Ok, kids, lighten up.
This is Mom's day.
For a little while let's be different
And do things her way.

Let's prove how much we love her
And start with breakfast in bed.
Not for you guys!!
This is for Mom instead.

Let's figure out a plan
For all day long so she
Doesn't have to work so hard
Like usual for you and me.

She deserves more than she asks.
With this, I am sure you'll agree.
Let's tell her and show her
The love each day she'd like to see.

SOUVENIRS

I have so many memories
From which I'll never part.
Cherished moments, Dad,
I carry in my heart.

Each one a souvenir
Of happiness and joy,
A gift of love from God
To a Father and his Boy.

I'll always love you, Dad,
For you have given me
These souvenirs to keep
Among my memories.

A BOUQUET FOR MOM

"Here, Mom, are some flowers,
I picked them just for you.
They were growing right next door,
And there's yellow, red and blue!"

Looking down at this little boy
With love shining from his eyes
I took his gift and held him close
So he wouldn't see me cry.

I placed them in my prettiest vase
And watched his young approval,
Wondering what to tell the neighbors
About their flowers' removal.

I didn't tell him at that moment
With his boyish face so bright,
That he shouldn't pick the neighbor's flowers
And we would have to make it right.

The folks next door forgave his deed,
For they had youngsters, too,
And understood a little boy's love
For yellow, red and blue.

A MOTHER'S DAY

She stood by the stove with flour on her face
Preparing the evening meal
And wondered out loud if later,
A few minutes rest she might steal.

She looked at the clock and quickly took stock
Of things there were yet to do.
Then with a big sigh finished making her pie
And put the lid back on the stew.

The sound of the vacuum filled every room
As the clutter she cleared away.
The furniture shone as she dusted,
Her house nice and clean for a day.

The baby was crying and had to be fed
While Junior was running around
Creating a mess wherever he went,
So quick and destructive, not making a sound.

She said, "I'm your poor tired mother,
Please don't do that to me.
Boy, when your father comes home
He'll make you behave, you'll see!"

The sound of a car in the driveway
And the front door opening wide
Brought a flush of love to her face
As she looked at her husband with pride.

"How was your day?" they said to each other
As they hugged with the kids in their arms.
And giggled and laughed about nothing at all,
Their problems no cause for alarm.

WIFE AND MOTHER

Hi Mama, I'm home!
How was your day?
Oh, Daddy, I'm so glad you're here.
I miss you in so many ways.

As usual it's been a busy day.
It seems there's always something to do...
Never a moment to rest
And dream about you.

The kids were busy as usual
And I sent them outside to play.
Our songs that I played soothed me,
As I cleared the clutter away.

Enough about me!
Are you tired, dear?
You work so hard
And I want you near.

I put your slippers by your chair
And the papers are there too.
Dinner will be ready soon
With things I made for you.

I love you, Honey, and I'm
Glad you're home.

DEAR DAD

Dear Dad,
Another day is ours,
One more page in the book of time.
The words of love already there
Are yours and mine.

Dear Dad,
Thank you for the love
That brightened all my days.
I will always care
More than words can ever say.

Dear Dad,
It's great to remember yesterday
And talk about tomorrow with you.
I wish you happiness and love.
May all your dreams come true.

Your Son

A FATHER'S LOVE

I can't imagine life
Without memories of my Dad
He made good things happen
No matter what we had.

We shared life's blessings together
He was a loving family man
Working so hard for all of us
His motto was "I can".

AND HE DID!
Always doing his best.
I will love you forever, Dad,
And wish you happy rest.

FATHERS' DAY

Happy Fathers' Day, Dear God,
Creator of our world.
We shall forever keep
The flag of faith unfurled.

Heavenly Father, we thank you
For your watchful care each day,
And for our mortal Dads,
A special love we pray.

On this special day for fathers,
How happy you must be,
To have your Son beside you,
As our world you oversee.

LOVE AND "THINGS"

When I talk to God
Would it be wrong for me
To call Him Dad?
I don't have one, you see.

Every child needs a father's love
To share "things" with each day.
I don't know what happened
But my real Dad went away.

I'd like to talk about "things"
That only fathers know.
Mom is wonderful
But Dad, I miss you so.

And so, God, my Heavenly Father,
If you wouldn't mind,
I'll call you "Dad" and share "things".
Mom says "you're good and kind".

MY FIRST FATHERS' DAY

I love you, Dad.
I'm too young to talk
And still too small
To hold your hand and walk.

I love you, Dad.
When asleep I know you're there,
My life is secure
Because you care.

I love you, Dad.
I'm going to grow, learn to talk,
I'll hold your hand
And take a walk.

I'll call you "DAD"
And then you'll know
How close we are –
I love you so.

CASTLE OF LOVE

Our house is my castle
And my Dad its King.
Each room is filled with sunshine
And the sound of laughter rings.

Each day is filled with happiness
And my Dad is always there
To help me conquer problems
With his tender loving care.

Love is the moat around my castle
And my Dad fills it for me.
He is the strength that keeps me safe
From things I cannot see.

I'll always remember our house
And my Dad reigning as King.
He taught me how to live
And gave me everything.

MY FATHER'S HAND

When I was little
And held my father's hand,
I wasn't afraid of anything,
The bravest in the land.

Dad's gentle touch gave comfort
His strength and love so strong
I knew that I was safe
And that nothing could go wrong.

He taught me how to walk
And on my own two feet to stand.
When I stumbled along the way
I had my father's hand.

I need our Heavenly Father
To help me through each day.
I have to hold His hand
Now that Dad has gone away.

MY DAD

A little boy was asked
What he would like to be
When he was grown-up
And had a college degree.

He smiled a wistful boyish smile
And said, "I'd like to be
Just like my Dad.
He made us a happy family."

"He isn't with us anymore
'cause Jesus loved him too
And wanted Dad in Heaven
Beyond the skies of blue".

"He was my friend, my Dad,
And nice to everyone, I believe.
Mom says she's glad we met
Before he had to leave."

"I guess if I could choose
The man I'd like to be
It would have to be "My Dad"
He loved the world and me."

YESTERDAY'S ETCHING OF A BOY AND HIS DAD

It was nearly bedtime and soft, fluffy snowflakes were falling. Our house was nice and warm from the wood burning stove glowing brightly and the additional light from the kerosene lamp. Home was a good place to be.

There was no school tomorrow…only chores…and that was enough for me. I dreamed of all the things I would rather do…a typical ten year old boy's ambition. I wanted to go hunting with my Dad and dogs. Small game was plentiful and Dad was the best…as were our hounds.

Almost like magic I heard Dad's voice saying, "Wanna go hunting in the morning?" Nice snow for tracking and the dogs need to go." Heaven opened up for me as I dived for bed…hoping for daylight soon.

I didn't need Dad's call to get out of bed, and after he fixed our breakfast, we were on our way with dogs crazy to hunt. Once we reached the woods and fields, the dogs began their chase of plentiful small game and the sound of their voices was a joy to hear.

As usual, Dad's shooting had no equal. Our quota of game filled, we headed for home and once again son and father were as one.

Trudging through the woods as we neared home, with the dogs running around, Dad noticed my feet were soaking wet and covered with snow. He asked if they were cold, and said, "I'm sorry, Son. Why didn't you say something?" (I wouldn't have spoiled this day if my feet were frozen!)

As close as we were to home, he called the dogs in and built a warm fire, removed my wet shoes and socks, placed them by the fire to dry, spread his coat on the ground and sat me down with bare feet toasting in the fire's warmth.

As we waited for my shoes to dry, a father and son's love, with devoted hunting dogs as witnesses, became permanently etched in time.

For my Dad with an eternity of love.

LOVE IS TIMELESS...FAMILY IS FOREVER

I held the telephone close...not wanting to miss one word...dreading the moment when our conversation would end...eager to hear every small detail about his new life away as he adjusted to being on his own...capable as always...searching for new horizons to conquer.

The words, "Goodbye, Dad, I love you", echoed through space and I closed my eyes to time and distance as I drifted into the vastness of yesterday and memories.

I watched time "fast forward"...each frame a memory, as a little boy ran into tomorrow with all the joy of life bouncing into the future unafraid.

I look at my grown up son and give thanks to our Heavenly Father for yesterday and memories. I know that He ran beside him and once again I hear his boyish laughter and feel the winds of time.

We still have our dreams. They have brought us to where we are. We are a loving family with faith and trust in God. For yesterday, today and all of our tomorrows, we thank Him.

REMEMBERING

Did you ever –

Squeeze mud through your toes
And enjoy the feeling
Of rain soaked clothes?

Wonder how fish could breathe
And what kept them warm
So they didn't freeze?

Watch birds in the sky
And wonder if feathers
Could make you fly?

Wonder why animals can't talk,
Why they have fur
And need four legs to walk?

Wonder what it might be like
To run against the wind
And fly a kite?

Of course you did,
If you'll just remember
You were once a kid!

SHADOWS

Your shadow is a copycat
Going everywhere with you,
But doesn't talk or make a sound
Doing everything you do.

Your shadow likes the sunshine
And will play outside with you
Until the sun goes down
Then disappears from view.

Shadows don't like darkness,
But when the moon is bright
They will suddenly appear
And hold your hand real tight.

At bedtime before "lights out"
Your shadow is "on-call"
And will perform for you
Upon your bedroom wall.

Your shadow is a copycat
That will always be with you
And forever be your Pal
No matter what you do.

TO MY CHILDREN ON FATHERS' DAY

Every day is "Fathers' Day"
I'm still watching what you do.
I couldn't ask for more
Than sharing a life with you.

I think about the past
With your Mother by my side,
Remembering all the fun we shared,
How you filled our hearts with pride.

Each day was an unknown challenge,
There was always something new.
We were a happy, loving family,
Your Mom and I and you.

I remember most of all, the laughter
That rang in every room,
The carefree sound of children
Singing out of tune.

The laughter is still there
And all our loving, too.
That's why every day is "Fathers' Day".
I'm so lucky to have you.

MY SON, MY SON

Let me hold you close,
And bridge the gap of time
To the miracle of birth,
And youthful days sublime.

I want to hold you close again,
And not have to share
The love of a son
Beyond compare.

I sit alone and wonder
What I might have done,
And find a world of happiness
In loving you, my son.

You are a part
Of everything I do,
That began so long ago
With my first glimpse of you.

What a wondrous love my son, my son,
I've found in what we two have done.

I'D LIKE TO BE A LITTLE BOY

I'd like to be a little boy
Maybe four or five years old
And know the wonders once again
Of the life a little boy holds

I want to sit on my mother's lap,
Wrestle with Dad on the floor,
Feel safe with their arms around me
And have their love once more.

I'd like to dream a child's dream
And be what I want to be...
To explore a world of imagination
That only I can see.

I'd like to go back for awhile
And relive my memories
Of happy days with Mom and Dad
And a little boy's fantasies.

TOO BIG

He doesn't hold my hand
When we walk
(He's too big!)

Seems like only yesterday
I carried him on my shoulders
And held both his hands.
(He was so small.)

He doesn't pay attention
To what I'm saying
But loves to talk.
(He's an expert on everything!)

Not yet grown
And still a little boy,
He'll always be my baby.
(I could never say so!)

I miss the baby,
Love my little boy
And dream of the man he'll be.
I won't ask that he hold my hand,
For he's too big, you see.

SHARING

I held the hand of my little boy
As he looked up at me
And asked if he could stay up late
To keep me company.

He knew that I was tired
And I heard him quietly say
"Let's talk about fishin', Dad,
And what we did today."

We shared our daily secrets
As the years sped swiftly by,
Just the two of us
That little boy and I.

At first I held him in my arms
And later side by side,
As he grew into a man
He filled my heart with pride.

I'll always remember that little boy
And forever hear him say,
"Let's talk about fishin', Dad
And what we did today".

TEARS

Two big eyes brimming with tears
And curly head turned away,
Not wanting to hear
What Dad had to say.
He shouldn't have done
The things he did,
But after all,
He's just a kid.
And then Dad whispered
Soft and clear,
"Don't cry son, there's nothing to fear".
He turned and leaped
Into outstretched arms...
Sobbing out his love,
All safe from harm.
He saw Dad's eyes
Fill with tears
And whispered soft and clear,
"Don't cry Dad, there's nothing to fear."

LIFE IS NOW

I found a heartache tucked away
So very long ago,
And held it up to search
For the pain I used to know.

The hurt has gone away
Its memory, oh, so dim.
Time has healed the wound
And I am whole again.

Growing old can be beautiful
And Life is now.
Hold it up and search for peace
Make happiness your vow.

A NEW AGE

Hands that show the passing of time
Are hands that toiled with love.
Eyes that crinkle when smiling
Reflect more than sunshine above.

The arches of your feet have fallen
Why worry about the hands?
You don't have to walk on them.
It's on your feet you stand.

Veins that carry your life's blood
All of a sudden you see
And excitedly ask
"Oh, boy, what has happened to me?"

Your hearing isn't exactly
What you remembered sound to be,
But then, who cares?
Sometimes this sets you free!

The years have gathered one by one
With all their memories.
Time brings tomorrow and happiness
Just you wait and see.

YOUNG AT HEART

Tell me about the old days
And the way life used to be,
Of dreams a young man had
Not knowing his destiny.

Tell me of the good times,
Don't talk about the sad.
Why worry over yesterday,
Or the wealth you might have had.

Light the flame of memory
And let the fire rage.
Remember the love and laughter
Written on every page.

Relive the chapters of your life
With happy memories
Forget the times of sadness
And young at heart you'll be.

AGE AND TRUTH

I sometimes miss the feeling
Of being young,
Miss that surge of youth
Resenting for a moment
The onset of Time,
Yet unafraid of age and truth.
And then again I wonder,
Do I really remember?
I was young so long ago.
I didn't appreciate youth then,
And would I now,
If given the chance to know?
I'm waiting for tomorrow
And the unknown joy
Another day might bring.
I wouldn't barter
The blessings I have
My age has made me a King.

ACHES AND PAINS

Woke up this morning
With the same old aches and pains.
Looked outside for sun
And all I saw was rain.

They say damp weather
Seems to bother you.
Even doctors agree
There's little you can do.

I put on a sweater, had my coffee,
Took a couple of pills
And felt sorry for the birds
Sitting on my window sill.

At least I was warm,
Comfortable and dry
Wishing that I had wings
And to sunshine I would fly.

Tomorrow is another day and
I know that I'll feel better,
If the sun would only shine
And the weather isn't wetter.

GROWING OLDER

There are faces and places,
Things I'm supposed to know
That fell through the cracks of memory.
Where did they all go?

I didn't always have this problem,
There was little I couldn't do.
Remembering came so easily
Because everything was new.

Now that I am older
Events from long ago
Have faded with the years
And my recall is so slow.

My life is filled with love,
I usually am just fine.
My memory needn't be so perfect –
I have so much that is mine.

AGEING

Age takes its toll.
This I know is true.
One doesn't want to believe
Until it happens to you.

A change in weather, for example,
Makes your joints ache.
"How can this be??", you ask
As your many pills you take.

Memory is another thing.
Where did it go?
I remember years past.
Don't ask about yesterday...I don't know!

And yet I plan for tomorrow
With the joy it might bring...
When God watches over you.
His love is everything.

31

BIG-FOOT

His little hand took mine
And he very politely said
"Come, Papa, come.
I have to go to bed.

I need you to read a story
Before I go to sleep.
You promised that you would
And a promise you have to keep.

I've had a bath, brushed my teeth
And did my homework too.
I have a book about a truck
I'd like to read with you.

"Big-Foot" is its name,
Nobody can beat this truck.
It's so huge and big,
Even in mud it don't get stuck!"

Page by page his excitement mounted.
His laughter filled the room
As "Big-Foot" crushed all the cars
And was their racing doom.

The race was over –
And every page recalled
With two sleepy eyes finally closing
On "Big-Foot" the greatest truck of all.

GRANDMOTHERS

Grandmothers are more than "Grand".
Their title is their fame.
Ask any child or grown-up
And the answer will be the same.

Grandmothers believe you're perfect.
Convinced you're never wrong,
Knowing without your talent
The world couldn't get along.

Grandmothers love to hug and kiss.
She doesn't care how old you are,
You're her greatest joy in life,
Her wonderful shining star.

Grandmothers know what children want,
And what grown-ups seem to need.
How lucky we are to have them
And their loving Grandmother deeds.

THE VISIT TO GRANDMA AND PAPA'S HOUSE

Smudges on each window pane,
Tiny handprints everywhere,
Crackers and jelly on the floor
With a toy left here and there.

The sound of little charging feet
Still echo in every room,
With memories of happy laughter
And kids that left too soon.

Scratches on the furniture
That were not there before
Enhance the beauty of each piece
And will stay for evermore.

The hardest part of memories
And yet the nicest thing,
Is remembering how their love felt
And the joy that they could bring.

It isn't easy to say good-bye,
Life just won't seem the same.
This hectic love is over
And you're so glad they came.

Each age is another time in life
For children to explore.
You just can't wait to join them
And hold them close once more.

GRANDMA'S BABY

As I held his precious little body
Close to mine, the wonders of
Heaven are revealed. How I wish
It could be this way forever!

He feels as light as a feather
On an angel's wing, as he lies in
My arms.

This smart, loveable, handsome baby,
By the will of God, is ours. I am
His Grandma, and I love him

He is such a good baby. See how he
Smiles and moves his tiny hands?

If he should cry when I am near,
I will gently rock him in my arms
Until he cries no more.

I know that he will grow and we
Will someday part, but I will
Always be his Grandma and he
Will always have my heart.

"HI, GRANDMA"

My three babies were boys
And I watched them grow
Filling my life with love
More than they'll ever know.

The early years passed swiftly
When it seemed they were mine alone...
Caring for their every need.
And suddenly, they were grown.

One by one they found another
And my happiness knew no bounds,
Rejoicing in the new love
My grown-up boys had found.

No one knew
How much I missed
A child's laughter
And the hurts I kissed.

God must have seen my lonely tears
And blessed me again and again,
Giving me four grandsons to love
As they grow up to be men.

Two little words more precious than gold
Brighten my every day
When I can hold them in my arms
And they hug me hard and say,
"Hi, Grandma!"

JUST DANDY

It's kinda hard anymore
To have that perfect day
When everything's "Just Dandy"
And going your way.

You need a warm sweater
To ward off the chill
And you can't remember
If you took your pills.

But you feel pretty good
Most all of the time
And your eyes still gleam
With that youthful shine.

You've learned to accept
Both the good and the bad
And change if you must
Without feeling sad.

There's always tomorrow
And another day
That could be "Just Dandy"
And going your way.

"STORE BOUGHT" BREAD

Remember when your school lunch sandwiches
Were made with homemade bread,
And how you wished they were made
With "store-bought" bread instead?

Remember the newspaper wrapped lunches
You tried so hard to hide
'cause you didn't have a lunch box
With "store-bought" bread inside?

Remember how the other kids
Were always willing to trade
'cause they never had a sandwich
With bread that was homemade?

Remember the lunch you carried to school
Wrapped in newspaper each day?
A mother's love, tied with string,
Cherished memories of yesterday.

DREAMS OF YOUTH

Time quietly slipped away
No longer witness to the dreams of youth,
And a young man was suddenly old,
Still searching, in his quest for truth.

My journey has been a wondrous one,
Sipping knowledge from Life's fountain.
Traveling with God's love and strength
As I sought to conquer my mountain.

The thought of conquest lingers,
Though not as strong.
My mountain of dreams is now a hill
And I know where I belong.

Time is witness to another age,
Unwilling to release its hold
While on the Stage of Life
Another act unfolds.

FAMILY DOG

He never was much of a dog...
More human, more like a kid,
And that's how he was treated
In everything he did.

He never liked to be alone.
Very few humans do,
And he would cry when you went away
'Cause he wanted to be with you.

He never asked for special care.
Love was his greatest hope,
And if it wasn't there
He'd lay around and mope.

A pat on the head just wasn't enough.
Only a hug would suffice.
He needed to be close
And feel like part of your life.

He isn't with us anymore.
He never wanted to leave.
But he'll be loved wherever he is.
In this I'll always believe.

SHARING

A little boy with boyish arm
around the neck of his dog sat in
the shade of a very large tree…sharing
an ice cream cone on a very hot day.

He would take a lick and his friend
pantingly watched…and then offered
the cone to him. As they eagerly
shared…lick for lick I was
witness to a rare bond of friendship.

The cone eaten, the grateful dog
wriggled with joy until I thought
he would fall apart trying to kiss
the face of this boy. Such love!!!

I thought of the joy sharing
our blessings with others could
bring and offered up a silent
prayer to our Heavenly Father
to guide me in the ways of
this little boy as he
unselfishly shared his wealth
with his friend.

God is good all the time.

STOLEN TREASURE

In the depths of our mind
Like the fathoms of the sea
Lurk unknown riptides
Unwilling to set us free.

Don't let the force
Of this monstrous undertow
Pull you away from life
And happiness you should know.

A guardian angel is near
To help you through each day
Reach out and take the hand
That God has sent your way.

Love is Life's greatest treasure
God meant for you to share.
He wouldn't place you here on earth
Without someone to care.

BIRTHDAYS

Tomorrow is my birthday but for
today I am still one year younger.
I am going to hold that youthful number
until time takes away the privilege.
I look forward to a new year that the
world has not yet seen and pray that God
will bless me with love and courage to
face the vagaries of time.
I cherish the birthdays past for they
have brought me where I am.
I still have my memories and dreams.

I NEED A FRIEND TODAY

If I ask you for a helping hand
Will you turn away
As though my problem didn't exist?
I need a friend today.

I'm lonesome – that's all...
And scared inside,
Is there no escape?
Must I always hide?

If only for a moment
You could help me find my way,
I'd be forever thankful.
I need a friend today.

The sound of laughter.
The quiet tear.
These I must share
To conquer fear.

I only ask that
You smile and say,
"I'll be your friend"
And not turn away.

FISHIN'

I'm just a guy that likes to go fishin'
Instead of laying around doing nothin' but wishin'

I took my pole down by the lake
And cast in the middle with my favorite bait.

It doesn't lay still in the water very long
'cause the current is fast and might strong.

I start to reel as fast as I can
And try to catch a fish for my frying pan.

I get a hit that feels mighty good
And I set the hook as best I could.

That fish on my line is huge and strong.
I know I'll have to fight him all night long.

I finally pulled that monster to shore.
He was so tired he couldn't fight anymore.

I looked at this fish and knew I'd won,
So I threw him back in just for fun.

THREADS OF LOVE

I thought that I could get along
All by myself, but I was wrong.

Close together or far apart,
Threads of love bind heart to heart.

This web of love makes my heart sing
With the joy of remembering.

I have another thread to weave into my life,
A beautiful princess who's going to be my wife.

She is the sweetest girl I have ever known,
44   And with a love like ours, I'll never be alone.

MEMORIES

I remember when I first called you sweetheart,
And I remember too,
When I first held you close,
And said that I love you.

Precious memories shrink the years,
And on this special day,
I thank you for the love
You gave me yesterday.

HAPPY BIRTHDAY, SON
A SPECIAL MOMENT IN TIME

Yesterday, today and tomorrow
Are only moments in time
That fade with the setting sun…
Each day a gift divine.
Your birthday will never fade.
A special moment in time
When our Heavenly Father said
"This gift of life is mine".
Praise Him above all others
For blessings given you.
Follow His guiding light
In everything you do.
As we celebrate your birthday,
May God's love follow you.
We add our faith to yours…
Each year a moment that's new.
There is no age in Heaven
Where we will someday be…
Just as God created us
For all eternity.
Happy Birthday, Son
On this special moment in time
When our Heavenly Father said,
"This gift of life is mine".
                    Love,
                    Dad

45

HAPPY SWEET SIXTEEN

Nothing can be said about "Sweet Sixteen"
That hasn't been said before...
Except today...this age is yours...
The "big one" you have waited for.

Precious "little girl" things
No longer rule the scene
With tears of happiness
Our "little girl" becomes "Sweet Sixteen".

Sixteen is the magic word
That opens so many doors
To the "grownup" dreams
You've been waiting to explore.

You excel in everything you do
And seek the joy that's there...
Loving what life has to offer...
Always willing to share.

Your family and loved ones
Are so proud of you!
May all your days be filled
With "grownup" dreams come true.

A TOAST TO FRIENDSHIP

We have been friends forever.
Out of sight at times, I know,
But never out of mine
No matter where we go.

God's greatest gift is someone
Who says, "I'll be your friend".
May we never know a day
When such an offer ends.

May our future hold much happiness...
May our friendships never stray
Until we gather again to share,
Let sunshine fill each day.

HAPPY RETIREMENT

There will always be another threshold...another door,
If you only have the courage to enter and explore.
Close the door softly when leaving the past.
Your future is now. May your happiness last.

THE BIG "5-0"

Over the hill and through the woods.
How do you get out?
Don't think about being fifty...
Pretend you're young and shout:

"A half century isn't so bad
With all that I have done.
The woods aren't really all that deep...
Just look how far I've come!

I have the next three dozen made...
And each one of them I'll share
With family and friends...my loved ones...
And may they always be there."

ENDLESS LOVE

I see my dream when I look at you.
No change is there.
You're the girl I fell in love with...
The fairest of the fair.

Happy birthday, darling.
No need to count the years.
Ours is an endless love...
Unmarred by time or tears.

47

SHIFTING SANDS

Footprints on Life's shores of knowledge
Remain unchanged by tides.
Their imprint lasts forever
As they take each change in stride.

One grain of sand helps build
The mighty ocean's shore.
The smallest act of learning
Leaves a mark forever more.

The world awaits your talent.
Be all that you can be
For you alone control the force
That shapes your destiny.

Face the tides of Life with pride
And to yourself be fair.
Leave footprints others want to follow
Remembering you were there.

Where will your footprints lead?
What will they reveal?
Will shifting sands whisper your name
As one whose dreams are real?

The Book of Life is a strange one.
No two volumes are the same
For each of us are authors
And we have no one else to blame.

BIRTHDAYS

A birthday is a new beginning
A time no one has seen before
So how could things go wrong?
It's like a brand new store!

Been there! Done that!
It seems there's nothing new.
Wanna bet? Well, don't!
There are surprises waiting for you.

Fifty isn't really different
Than any other year.
Another journey is starting…
Forget the tales you hear.

Did someone say half-century?
How could fifty be so long?
It seems like only yesterday-
But that's another song.

Age is only a figure.
Life's treasures are in your heart.
May you be blessed with happiness
And each year be a joy to start!

BEST FRIEND

The words of trust we've shared together
Through all our years
Have been filled with happiness
And sometimes tears.

Threads of caring spun by God
Bind heart to heart
And give a special meaning
To each day's start.

You are in my thoughts
And never far away.
Walk with our Savior, Jesus,
He is the sunshine in each day.

"What a friend we have in Jesus"
Are words so old, yet new…
And I believe with all my heart
Because he gave me you.

Happy Birthday, dear friend.

TIME

Yesterdays have changed to years.
Tomorrow is a dream to share.
Every today is special
And you wonder if time is fair.

There will always be memories.
Don't dwell on sadness and tears.
Choose the happy ones
And fill your life with cheer.

Look to tomorrow!
Dreams sometimes do come true
And with God's help and faith
Time will be fair to you.

HAPPY BIRTHDAY, BROTHER

I searched the town and others nearby
To find you a birthday card,
But try as I might I had no luck.
Lord knows I tried awfully hard.

Verse after verse I eagerly read
In search of words to explain
How someone as old as my brother
Could be so outrageously vain.

Age doesn't lie on the calendar.
They say it's all in the mind.
Too bad your memory is fading
And so I'll try to be kind.

Happy birthday, brother, I love you,
And wouldn't think of mentioning years.
I hope you can read my best wishes
Through your bi-focals and many tears.

HAPPY BIRTHDAY!

Birthdays are fun days
No matter your years.
Age makes no difference
When loved ones are near.

Each year is God's gift
When He stayed by your side...
Each step a journey of love
As He walked as your guide.

Give thanks for birthdays past
And raise a glass with friends,
For the promise of tomorrow
And a love that never ends.

GOD'S BIRTHDAY GIFT

Fifty six years isn't nearly as long
As I imagined it would be.
I thank you, Lord, for every year
And the blessings given me.

I have walked each day with Jesus.
Yes, he's been right by my side...
And step by step he's always been
My loving, faithful guide.

There have been some crisis moments,
But I was never left alone,
And knew that with his guiding light
I would find my way back home.

I have friends...a loving family...
God's gift to show His care,
Tomorrow's a new beginning
And I know He will be there.

BIRTHDAYS

Birthdays mark the passing of time.
Each year a flower in life's bouquet.
As the petals in each blossom unfold
We're given the wonders of another day.

The beauty of life revealed
And the treasures that you hold
Make each age the sweetest story
That time has ever told.

Remember the flowers given you
As their petals softly fall.
Memories bloom around them...
Each one the best of all.

KINDERGARTEN SWEETHEART

She would help me with
My boots, coat, hat and gloves...
Kiss me lightly and send me home...
Hopelessly in love.

She was my kindergarten teacher...
The prettiest woman in my life
And I couldn't wait to grow
So she could be my wife.

I never told her
But I think she knew.
She set a standard for me
I would carry my whole life through.

Happy Valentine's Day to a memory
Of a young boy's teacher love...
The beauty and innocence of a childhood.
God's gift from Heaven above.

OUR KITCHEN CALENDAR

The calendar on our kitchen wall
Reveals more than a month and day
It's a family diary of important dates
That's always on display.

Each day of every month
Is printed on large squares
So that memories and planning can be recorded there.

It's an amazing journal
A history of the past
And a reminder of events to come.
Time slips away so fast.

Family and friends feel the heartache
And see the quiet tear
Or share the happiness noted
Each day throughout the year.

Our calendar grows more precious
With every passing day.
The sunshine in its pages
Time can never take away.

HANDS OF LOVE

We will never forget
Our little girl baby
And how she became
Our grown-up lady.

How she gripped
Our fingers with her tiny hands,
And our hearts with a love
She didn't yet understand.

How proud we were
When she learned how to stand,
Holding our dreams
In the palm of her hand.

Reaching up-
With arms held high
So eager to conquer
What ever met the eye.

We were pals holding hands,
Learning how to share.
One needing the other,
And always there.

And then one day she let go our hands
To try and walk alone,
Like a little bird eager to fly
Though she had never flown.

Now that she has found
Another hand to hold,
We wish her love,
And a rainbow's pot of gold.

PARTNERS

I want to say "I love you"
In a very special way – my way

I want to share with you all the
Dreams of man – since time began,
A woman – A wife – A mother.

A partner in life – to live, love
And share.

To create life beyond compare –
Our way.

STOLEN LOVE

A tiny flame flickers
In the ashes of love seeking warmth
As dying embers explode and dreams disappear.

One by one each little spark
That warmed two hearts has gone.
Love's flame extinguished by tears.

Hidden in a lonely heart
Stolen love can never be shown.

Lost are the happy days
When love is not your own.

LOVE'S CHOICE

We will always remember
The sound of your voice,
Soft and clear,
Announcing your choice.

"Mom and Dad, he wants to marry me,
And I've agreed.
I love him,
And he answers my heart's need."

Too soon the time had come
When we were to hear,
There was someone special
You wanted near.

We never realized
Our baby girl had grown,
Prepared to face life's challenges
On her own.

The years have slipped away,
We still have your carriage.
It seems like only yesterday
And now you're ready for marriage.

Tears of joy and sadness
Make memories more clear
Of our grown-up baby
And the precious years.

We wish you happiness
As you share
Your life and dreams
With another who cares.

Though you're gone,
We will never be apart,
For you will always be
Our baby girl, sweetheart.

FROM A DAUGHTER TO HER MOTHER

Tears of happiness, Mom
Bring memories so clear
Of your tender love
And having you so near.

Through laughter and tears
Close together or far apart
The threads of love
Bind heart to heart.

This web of love
Makes my heart sing.
With a family like ours
I have most everything

There is another thread
To weave into my life
A very special person
Who wants me for his wife.

He answers my heart's need
Now that I am grown
And with a love like ours
I will never be alone.

Mom, although I've found
Another hand to hold
Your love will always be
My Rainbow's Pot of Gold.

HAPPY BIRTHDAY,
GILBERT IEM
SEPTEMBER 7, 2007

Another year…
Another time…
Another birthday
For a special friend of mine.

More than a friend—
As stars are to Heaven
And sunshine to each day…
He is a special gift
That God has sent our way.

He scatters his love
Wherever he goes…
Never finding fault…giving praise.
He is so special to know.

No burden too heavy
For him to share
Turn to him in need.
He is always there.

Such a capable man…
Husband, father and friend.
To know him is to love him.
His caring never ends.

Thank you God for Gil,
Bud Gray

FREEDOM WARRIOR

Out of the ashes of war's destruction
The Phoenix of Freedom is born
Seeking the help of warriors
For a country ravaged and torn.

Our warrior son joined the ranks
To fight in Vietnam
And endure the fires of hell
Unleashed by man and bomb.

The Phantoms of peace and destruction
That flew the jungle sky
Were kept aloft by caring hands
That prayed no one would die.

His was a mission of freedom
A sacrifice of love
For the right of others to live
As taught by God above.

He fought with the brave
Youthful freedom fighters supreme
Doing what their nation asked
Of the United States Marines.

He gave his heart to the battle
The fighting at last was done
Our warrior son survived
To ask what had they won?

The bells that toll for freedom
Shall forever and ever ring
For those who seek the dream
It promises to bring.

MILLER, INDIANA
BY RAYMOND (BUD) GRAY
JULY 23, 2005

I want to go back home again
To visit yesterday,
But time has changed so many things
And I have lost my way.

I want to see old faces,
Hear voices I once knew.
Walk down Memory Lane once more
And live those days anew.

I want to go back to Miller, Indiana,
But only in my dreams…
To youthful, carefree, happy days
And quiet small town scenes.

I want to be a kid once more…
Go to Jack-Spratts for a "nickel" cone…
Visit "Ma Todd's" for some penny candy…
And be safe just walking home.

I want to swim and fish at Carr's Beach…
Swim at the B.A.B. on the lagoon -
Do all the things of yesterday
That time has ended too soon.

I want to go back to Miller, Indiana
Where each day was a joy to live,
But only in my dreams,
For I have no youth to give.

BACK HOME IN MILLER...
SUBURB OF HEAVEN

They say you can't go "home" again.
In many ways this is true,
But let's turn back time to Miller
And yesterday with you.

Some remember Miller as the place
Where they were born and lived,
Sharing with others family love
And all they had to give.

Others came, as families moved
To this suburb of Heaven they'd found.
There were no strangers in Miller
All were God's children...earth bound.

The games and laughter shared,
The helping hand we knew
Were a part of yesterday in Miller
And still belong to you.

They say, you can't go "home" again.
But in a moment you are there,
Just close your eyes and remember-
Miller, the suburb of Heaven we share.

"BACK HOME"

We can go "back home" again.
Makes no difference what others say.
Home is where the heart is
With memories of yesterday.

As you watch the setting sun,
Gather evening shadows 'round.
Give your burdens to God
And cherish memories that abound.

Remember your last reunion "back home"
And all who gathered there.
They are the magic you seek…
Life's treasure beyond compare.

The sound of forgotten youthful voices
Roll away the years
And time gives way to memories
As familiar faces appear.

Let's go "back home" again,
Reminisce with family and friends.
Touch the presence of those no longer here…
In this place where happiness never ends.

HELLO, MILLER…
WE HAVE COME "BACK HOME"!!!

MILLER REUNION 2007

THERE'S A BOND WE SHARE
WITHIN OUR "MILLER HEARTS",
NO MATTER WHERE WE ARE
WE WILL NEVER BE APART.

LIFE IS BEAUTIFUL
WHEN YOU CAN SAY
YOU LIVED IN MILLER, INDIANA...
FOR A SHORT TIME OR TO STAY.

PRESSED BETWEEN PAGES OF MEMORIES
ARE WONDERFUL "MILLER DAYS"...
A RECORD OF OUR GROWING-UP
WHEN LIFE WAS NOT A MAZE.

AS WE SAVOR THE THRILL OF YESTERDAY
WE ADD ANOTHER PAGE
TO OUR BOOK OF MEMORIES,
TOGETHER AGAIN...IN ANOTHER AGE.

THE YEARS HAVE DWINDLED DOWN
AND OUR NUMBERS GROW EVER SLIM.
OLD FRIENDS EMBRACE EACH OTHER
AS THEY GATHER ONCE AGAIN.

THERE IS ANOTHER HOME LIKE MILLER
WAITING WAY UP IN THE SKY...
WHERE LIFELONG FRIENDS COME HOME AGAIN
AND NEVER SAY GOODBYE.

HOME ADDRESS – SIXTY-FIVE NINETEEN

I want to go back home again
To visit yesterday,
But time has changed so many things
And I have lost my way.

Home was very special
We were all together then,
But I am older now
And my baby boys are men.

I want to hear them answer
My loving, worried call,
To hold my little boys once more
For that was best of all.

At times, I get so lonesome
And they're not near to share
My memories of their growing-up.
How I wish we all were there.

I want to go back home again,
But only in my dreams,
To carefree days of happiness
At our sixty-five nineteen.

SECTION TWO:
LOVE

MY WORLD IS YOU

I can't recapture moments past
Except in memory.
The ones I cherish most, my dear,
Are the ones you shared with me.

You grow more beautiful
With every passing year,
And for your loving care,
I cherish you, my dear.

Time has endowed us
With a love that's deep and true.
My world would surely stop
If I didn't have you.

GOOD MORNING, DARLING

Good morning, darling,
Awake to another day
While I hold you in my arms
And kiss the sleep away.

Good morning, darling,
What a day it's going to be.
The world is bright and sunny
'Cause my darling's here with me.

Good morning, darling,
As we lay side by side
A glance – A touch
Brings love we cannot hide.

I am so very thankful
For all our yesterdays.
I will dream about tomorrow
But I love you most today.

BEYOND TOMORROW

I will love you until the day after tomorrow,
That's one day longer than forever.
My happiness is sharing yesterday with you,
Loving memories of our time together.

I love you from the moment
The sun opens your sleepy eyes,
Until you fall asleep again
'Neath moonlit, starry skies.

I love you as you lay
Next to my caring heart,
For you are mine forever
And we shall never part.

TOGETHER

In the early morning darkness
With my eyes open wide,
I offer up a silent, thankful prayer
That you're sleeping by my side.

Abandoned by sleep,
My mind begins to roam
And I gently take your hand
So I won't be alone.

Reality and fears are jumbled,
Mixing smiles and tears
Until I fall asleep again---
My world is safe because you're near.

I STILL HAVE YOU

The night displayed a beauty
We never before had seen
As heart to heart we stood
And life became a dream.

Holding hands we walked
Among the stars
While angels sang a love song
And the world was ours.

We stole a bit of Heaven
To keep through all the years
And even now the angels sing
For I still have you, Dear.

REMEMBER TODAY

Remember loving and living life our way?
When nothing was greater than today?

Remember the happiness our love brought?
What a beautiful world we both sought?

We're still together and have today
With loving memories of yesterday.

LOVE'S REFLECTION

I remember the lass,
And the looking glass
Reflection of our love.

A loving wife
Betrothed for life,
In the presence of God above.

Sweetheart, Wife and Mother,
I love you more
Than any other.

WHEN YOU'RE IN LOVE

When someone loves you
And you love that someone too,
Two hearts entwine and beat as one;
I love you, I love you, I love you.

Not yet defined by the wisest sage,
Love is sweet at any age.
The sky above is a deeper blue,
The world more beautiful because of you.

IF I COULD

If I could steal the moments past,
I'd wipe away each tear
To give you happiness and love
Each day of every year.

If I could steal tomorrow,
Do you know what I would do?
I'd tie it 'round our hearts
And spend my life with you.

THIS IS MY HAPPINESS

A glance that says you love me
A touch that shows you care
And words with special meaning
That only lovers share---
This is my happiness.

A life together, just you and I
Is the dream that I have found.
May this love be ours forever
And your happiness know no bounds---
This is my happiness.

HAPPY LOVE

Another year is ours,
One more page in the Book of Time.
We've shared sunshine and starlight,
Precious moments that were yours and mine.

I can't remember all our years
But those I do recall
Were filled with happiness
Each one the best of all.

As we turn the pages
Our life unfolds
With all the love
Our hearts can hold.

ENDLESS LOVE

I see my dream when I look at you.
No change is there.
You're the girl I fell in love with,
The fairest of the fair.

Happy Birthday, Darling,
No need to count the years.
Ours is an endless love
Unmarred by time or tears.

DID I RUN AWAY

Did I run away from you,
Or did I run away from me?
I didn't understand,
Our love was meant to be.

Was I afraid of love,
Or was I afraid of me?
I never took the time
To face reality.

And now with every tear
I know I'll always love you, dear.

If I came running back to you,
Would you still care and love too?
Or would you run away,
Afraid that I would never stay?

TOMORROW'S DREAM

I thank you for the tenderness
Your love for me has shown.
My darling, you've brought me happiness
That I have never known.

You have stolen my heart.
What more can I say?
I'll dream about tomorrow,
But love you more today.

YOU WERE MEANT FOR ME

If you could peek into my heart
You'd see that you are there
And know that you're the one
Whose life I want to share.

If I could hold you in my arms
Then heart to heart we'd be.
And all the world would know
That you were meant for me.

YOU ARE MY LIFE

I want to hold you in my arms,
Until I'm sure you know
That every moment we're apart,
My love for you will grow.

You are my life,
And have given me
A world I thought
Could never be.

There are no words
For me to say
How much I love you
Every day.

73

BOY IS SHE PRETTY!

Boy, is she pretty!
That's how I described you
Before we ever met
And found our love so true.

I fell in love
With a beautiful, dark-eyed, tiny girl.
To me she was perfect
And became my world.

Your youthful body put to shame
The slender weeping willow -
Your beauty out of place
Not sleeping on my pillow.

My world became a castle
And you its Heavenly Queen.
The day you said, "I love you"
God gave me all my dreams.

Love,
Today, tomorrow and always

DREAM OF LOVE

She nestled in my arms
And I touched her lips with mine
To sip the thrill of happiness,
Lost in the kiss of an angel's wine.

Tears spilled from our cup of love
And I wiped them gently away
As we promised to love each other
Forever and a day.

The words "I love you" awakened me
And in the darkness I was alone
My face wet with tears
That were my own.

74   My darling, I love you

LASTING LOVE

You offered dreams.
I gave you truth
And our love endured
The passions of youth.

We gave our trust, one to the other,
To keep through all the years,
So that we would stay together
And conquer all our fears.

You're still the dream
You have always been
And I love you now
As I did then.

NO MORE TEARS

Bring me your lonely hours
And let me help you smile.
Share with me the dreams
That make your life worthwhile.

I want to hold you close
And keep you by my side,
Forever loved and happy
Forgetting when you cried.

A KISS

There's a kiss for hello
And a kiss for goodbye,
A kiss for happiness
Each one with a sigh.

There's a kiss for sorrow
And a kiss of regret,
A kiss for memories
We'll never forget.

The sweetest kiss is one of love
With someone close to your heart
As you embrace each other
And vow you'll never part.

SWEETHEART

If you will be my lady,
I will be your beau.
I want you for my sweetheart,
Because I love you so.

Take my heart and hold my hand,
Together we'll always be.
Life couldn't offer more
Than sharing it with thee.

I love you.

I WANT YOU HOME AGAIN

I want you home again
Back where you belong.
I can't live without you
And I know that I've done wrong.

I'm asking for another chance
To prove that I love you,
For without you by my side,
I don't know what to do.

I didn't mean to hurt you,
Didn't intend to do you harm.
Never thought about the heartache
Of another in your arms.

I can't replace your beauty,
Or the love that we once had.
I can't believe we're finished,
Can't get over feelin' bad.

I want you home again,
Back where you belong,
I'll always love you darlin'
And I'm sorry I've done wrong.

A TOAST TO LOVE

It really doesn't matter
How or where,
A boy and girl in love decide
Each others life to share.

Perhaps a glance or touch
Released the love inside,
Spilling over with feelings
They could no longer hide.

They're together at last
And stand before us now,
Promising each other eternal love
As they make their marriage vow.

A toast to lovers
Now joined as one -
"May they always cherish
The heart they've won".

THE MAGIC OF LOVE

Fragile moments that needed mending,
Aching hearts that needed tending,
Were made whole
With the Magic of Love.

Cloudy skies filled with rain,
Tearful eyes reflecting pain,
Were made clear
With the Magic of Love.

Two hearts skipped a beat,
A boy and girl wasting moments sweet,
Were made one
With the Magic of Love.

The impossible dream that you would care,
The impossible scheme our lives to share,
Were made real
With the Magic of Love.

STARTING OVER

Hello Darling, how have you been?
I miss you every day.
I'm sorry that I hurt you
And need so much to say-

If I could start all over
It would have to be with you.
You've changed my life forever
And no one else will do.

I remember when we said goodbye,
How you turned and walked away.
I knew that I had lost you
And had no words to say.

There's a look about you now,
I thought I'd never see.
Your beauty has stolen my heart again
And set my spirit free.

If we could start all over
And begin our lives anew,
Our love for one another
Would make my dreams come true.

LOST LOVE

I thought about yesterday
And how things might have been.
You haven't said you love me
Since I can't remember when.

There was a time for us
When all the world was ours.
We needed one another
and measured time by hours.

The years have taken their toll
And we've somehow drifted apart.
The love that we once had
Is a memory in my heart.

I wish you happiness
And a love forever true.
We were never meant to be.
There's someone waiting for you.

YOU WERE MEANT FOR ME

If you could peek into my heart,
You'd see that you are there
And know that you're the one
Whose life I want to share.

If I could hold you in my arms
Then Heart to Heart we'd be
And all the world would know
That you were meant for me.

RAINDROPS AND TEARS

You were a dream
Shining in the mist.
Raindrops reflecting your beauty,
As we embraced and kissed.

Holding you close,
Not wanting to cry,
I couldn't believe
You were saying goodbye.

I hear your laughter in the rain,
And you're not there.
You left me for another,
But I will always care.

Raindrops on my window pane
Make me blue.
For they remind me of a love
That I once knew.

We loved but for a moment
And parted in the rain,
Leaving me with tears
To wash away the pain.

DREAMS

I sailed the ship of Morpheus
On a dark and tranquil sea
To dream the dreams of make believe
And not reality.

My world became a crystal ball
And I a stately king
Surrounded by life's treasures...
Possessing everything.

Except the one I cherish most...
My loving, faithful wife.
My fantasies are worthless if
She can't share my life.

And so I've turned to daydreams...
A world of constant bliss
Where I can be awakened
By her sweet loving kiss.

THE BRIGHTEST STAR

I followed moonbeams to the sky
And plucked the brightest star.
I brought you back to earth with me...
And angel from afar.

You are the soft caress of a gentle breeze
With the warmth of a sunset's gold...
The promise of eternal love.
My heart you'll always hold.

You are my heavenly queen
And I your earthly king.
Together we shall reign...
Possessing everything.

WORDS OF LOVE

You have the warmth of sunshine in your eyes...
The romance of moonglow in your hair...
Your lips have the softness of rose petals
With fragrance that angels splashed there.

Your face has the blush and freshness of dawn.
You are so lovely and fair...
A picture of heaven's magical wonders
With the promise of love beyond compare.

Take my hand and hold my heart...
Together we will always be.
Life could not offer more
Than sharing it with thee.

THREADS OF LOVE

Distance is no barrier to caring.
Close together...or far apart
Threads of love
Bind heart to heart.

This web of love
Makes our hearts sing
With the joy of your friendship...
And remembering.

It isn't easy to say "goodbye"
And from you, dear friends, to part.
So just for now---"so long"...
And God bless you on your new start.

You will never be far away.

A KISS

Her lips, like a soft, warm summer breeze
Laden with the perfume of beauty, touched mine
And for one magical moment
A bit of Heaven stopped time.

A fleeting kiss
Like the touch of an angel's wing
Brushed my heart
And I heard a thousand bells ring.

There's a kiss for hello,
And a kiss for goodbye
A kiss of love
Each one with a sigh.

Of all the kisses
We sometimes give
The one that captures your heart
Makes life a joy to live.

LOVE PEEKED INTO MY HEART

Love peeked into my heart
And found you hiding there.
I didn't mind the intrusion
My secret I needed to share.

Love stole my heart that day
And gave it all to you,
My secret wasn't secret anymore
For finally you knew.

The words "I love you"
Aren't the easiest to say,
For they are a promise
You can never take away.

Love peeked into my heart
Then moved right in with you,
At last we were together
To each other forever true.

SHATTERED DREAMS

Shattered dreams...like shards of glass
Reflect the fantasy that once was there,
And as I carefully sweep them away
My heart is once more bare.

Except for one tiny splinter,
No one will ever see...
Reflecting a picture of beauty
And a dreamer's fantasy.

Life is reality and not a dream...
The elusive unreachable star,
And yet, when I close my eyes,
My darling, there you are.

And so I have turned to daydreams...
A world of constant bliss,
The splinter in my heart a memory
Of an angel's loving kiss.

AFTERNOON NAPS

Afternoon naps are to rest
And perhaps dream
Of distant shores of happiness
No one has ever seen.

A place that holds the joy
A make believe world might bring...
Where peace and love are wealth
And there is no suffering.

No matter what the dream
Or wealth I might possess,
Without you by my side
I would have no happiness.

Dreams are only dreams,
And you, my dear,
Are the only one
That I want near.

85

MY SECRET LOVE
WEAVER OF DREAMS

Weave me a cloak of love
To wear 'round my heart.
You are my beautiful world of make believe...
The sunshine of each day's start.

Let each thread be of happiness
For all you have given me.
In all my dreams you are real...
The woven love of fantasy.

Though only in my dreams
You often come to me.
My life is filled with a love
I thought could never be.

You may leave my arms,
But we will never part
For weaver you have stolen
The fabric of my heart.

LOVING WORDS

Loving words are the fuel
Feeding the flame in my heart...
Burning with faith and hope that
We will never be apart.

Tell me that you love me.
I need to hear you say
That neither one of us
Can take this love away.

Let me hear you whisper
The words that make you mine,
"I am yours forever.
Your love is my sunshine."

There is no beginning or end.
Our love was meant to be.
We two belong together.
86 Husband and wife, our destiny.

SILLY LOVE

I never thought I'd find a girl
That I could love so much -
A bashful one that giggled
And felt so good to touch.

Holding hands is what I mean
And maybe a hug or two.
'Cause she didn't believe in silly love
Her kisses were taboo.

I courted her with all my heart
In school and "growed-up", too.
Even though she giggled
And her kisses were taboo.

Holding hands in the parlor
I asked her to be my bride.
Two little tears rolled down her cheeks
As she stood there by my side.

She looked at me and giggled
Then blew a kiss or two,
Saying she'd believe in silly love
When she heard me say "I do".

SOMEONE SPECIAL

A toast my dear for memories
From which I'll never part.
For you are a special dream
I carry in my heart.

I was your football hero,
You were my pom-pon queen,
And the game we played was a timeless one,
Of youthful loving dreams.

Fate's interception changed the game
And our lives were never to be the same.

I hear the echo of your voice
With cheers meant just for me,
And I try a little harder
To fulfill my destiny.

To steal a moment of your time
Is a very secret play,
In this crazy game of life
As we go our separate ways.

May your game be a winner,
And this time I'll cheer
The champ I lost –
One yesteryear.

LOVIN' AIN'T EASY

I stopped with my friends
For a couple of beers,
Then hurried straight home
To a house without cheer.

My woman was gone
The table was bare
With no supper waiting
And no lovin' to share.

A note on the fridge
Said "So long, my dear,
I hope you enjoy
Your friend and the beer.

I'm tired of waiting
For you to come home,
While night after night
The town taverns you roam.

Don't try to find me
'less you want me to stay
By showing you care
And not drink every day.

I'll always love you
But you don't need me.
You just need a beer
And your friend's company."

After reading her note
I started to cry
And knew that without her
I surely would die.

I made a promise
I've kept through the years.
There's been no more drinking
No sorrow and tears.

It took me a while
To prove that I cared,
But I did – and she did
With a love we both shared.

BEST FRIEND

The words of trust we've shared together
Through all our years
Have been filled with happiness
And sometimes tears.

Threads of caring spun by God
Bind heart to heart
And give a special meaning
To each day's start.

You are in my thoughts
And never far away.
Walk with our Savior, Jesus.
He is the sunshine in each new day.

What a friend we have in Jesus
Are words so old, yet new,
And I believe with all my heart
Because he gave me you.

SECTION THREE:
NATURE

SEASONS OF LIFE

The onset of age with the hush
Of falling snow has brought
Another season of life, its
Silence broken only by the crunch
Of time beneath our feet.

The springtime of youth
And summer's middle age glow
Give way to change
As the winds of time blow.

RHYTHM OF LIFE

The rhythm of life can be found
In a babbling brook flowing free
Through mossy rocks and leaves...
Whispering to the grass and trees.

Gurgling with a happy sound
Of peace and tranquility...
A steady beat of joy
Sounding the call of eternity.

From the breast of Mother Earth
Springs eternal love.
With every beat of our heart
We flow closer to our Father above.

A NEW DAY

I wrapped the night around me,
And thought of morning, with all the joy
A new day might bring,
Sunshine and flowers,
A warm soft shower,
The beautiful sound as songbirds sing.

93

DUSK

The setting sun has tinged the sky
A beautiful pink, creating a blanket
Of colorful shadows.
As the quiet of dusk comforts
And soothes bringing tranquility,
We are given a special gift of Peace.

A LITTLE BOY'S CONQUEST

The shadow of a giant tree
Lay at my feet...felled by the
Rising sun. As a little boy
I scampered up its length and
Touched its crown.

As the sun moves on to conquer other
Giants and cast their silhouettes
Upon the earth, it gently lifts
My tree upright again and I can
Say that I, at last, have climbed
To its very top! Victory was mine.

JANUARY

January has been true winter
With no hint of spring.
There has been no "January thaw"
But today I heard a songbird sing.

Ice and snow in the birdbath
Melted in the warmth of the sun
And it was filled with bathing birds
As I watched with envy their fun.

The maple tree filled with robins,
A beautiful springtime bird,
Then without a sound they vanished.
Their silent beauty I saw and heard!

For a moment I was blessed
With the beauty of spring...
Surrounded by winter's grandeur
Thank you, God, for all these things.

THE BEAUTY OF SPRING

The wintry blast took one last fling
And ice and snow covered everything.
The chilling wind howled with glee
Whistling, "You're not yet rid of me!"
But then a warming breeze did blow
And melted winter's ice and snow.
Birds that flew from warmer climes
Were waiting for the sun to shine.
Spots of color in early bloom
Help chase away winter's gloom.
Sun and sky are warm and clear,
The beauty of spring will soon be here.

NIGHT AND DAY

Sir Night dons his sequined velvet cloak
And escorts the beautiful Miss Day to another date.

Knowing they can't stay together,
And each must go their separate way.

They will follow one another forever,
Accepting their earthly fate.

MAGNIFICENT TREE

In a barren field held captive
By the wire fence surrounding it,
A beautiful, magnificent tree stood
Alone...raising its limbs in praise
To God, Creator of all things.
A teasing summer breeze rustled
Through its dress of leaves creating
Splashes of sunlight on a cool
Blanket of shade on the ground
Beneath its boughs...inviting me
To tarry and rest awhile.
Lying on my back in the comfort
Of its embrace, I gave thanks
To our Heavenly Father for this
Magnificent tree. With bits
Of feathered color darting
Round and the symphony of sound
Beyond compare, I closed my
Eyes and drifted into its peace.

SEASONS OF LIFE

Our sugar maple tree in the backyard
After the rain, cold weather and storm
Is a picture of golden beauty...
With color so grand and warm.

The sunshine filtering through its leaves
Reflects the beauty of fall...
As the wonders of nature change,
Each season the best of all.

Thank you, dear Lord, for the beauty
You have given me
And I await the glory of heaven
That blooms eternally.

THE RESTLESS SEA

The sea leaping high
In anticipation of change
Pounds its unrelenting shores,
Roaring in frustration at being confined.
Pulled by an unseen force
It recedes, hissing in anger
Then thrusts again and again
Forever moving, never content.
On high the changing heavens
Reveal an ever-present moon
Smiling as it looks down
Upon the oceans of the earth
Moving to her commands,
Content in sharing the power
Controlling our world.

LITTLE BIRD LOST

It was a glimpse of motion
And a slight thud
Against the outside glass
Of the picture window.

A small bird with fluttering wings
That would never
Beat in flight again,
Fell lifeless to the ground.

A little fluff of feathers
Blown by the wind
Left its mark on the glass
Like a dusting of colors

On the palette of life,
To be washed away
By the rain-
Forever lost.

Only the memory of song
And beauty in flight remain,
With a prayer of thanks
For the joy they gave.

AUTUMN

The man in the moon on a clear fall night
Bathes the world with a crisp magic light
Brushing the earth with silvery beams
Creating a canvas of beautiful dreams
Then fades from sight with the light of day
Leaving his painting on display
Dusted with glittering diamonds, so rare,
Autumn's gift from nature
Sprinkled with care.

THE BEAUTY OF A TREE

One last leaf refused to fall
And so preserved the beauty of a tree
As it raised gnarled, barren branches high
For everyone to see.

It soon would wear a tiara of snow...
A robe of frosty white
That glistens in the sunshine
And sparkles through the night.

With majestic grandeur
It stands naked over-all
Except for one leaf proudly waving
That had refused to fall.

COME FLY WITH ME

In the early morning light
I heard a songbird's trill
And saw a fluff of feathers
Sitting on my window sill,

As if to say, "Wake up,
Another day is here.
The sun will soon be shining
In a sky so blue and clear.

Come fly with me in sunbeams
And let your spirit soar.
Leave earthly fears behind you
And find peace forevermore".

CANVASBACK DAWN

They come in quietly with the dawn
Flying low over the cattails
Searching for an opening to rest and feed
Gliding on winds fixed like feathered sails.

Scattered splashes reveal their landing
In water reflecting the blackness of night
The rising sun joins Heaven and Earth
As they end their weary flight.

The quiet of nature settles 'round
As they rest in water clear -
A refuge for all the waterfowl
In their migration every year.

This is a canvasback dawn
That few are privileged to see -
A glimpse of God's creation
Where peace should always be.

CHANGE

Gray skies hide the heaven's blue. The air
Is cold and damp, unwarmed by sunshine, as
It heralds the coming of fall.
The blowing rain brings a forgotten
Discomfort and thoughts of icy blasts
Soon to follow.

The season's first fire in the fireplace
Brings the pungent smell of wood smoke
Inside the house and conjures dreams
Of a harvest of beauty. The anticipation
Of events that only this time of year can
Bring stirs excitement.

An early frost covers the rooftops and
Grass with a silvery blanket that
Glistens in the morning sun as flowers
Shrink from the unfamiliar touch.

A rainbow of colors flows from the magical
Palette of Mother Nature touching the
Earth and splashing upward to the
Highest leaf on the tallest tree...
Bathing the countryside in glorious
Breath taking wonder.

Beauty follows beauty and one by one
Rich colors fade to be replaced by the
Blue, white cold of ice and snow with
The grandeur of a winter sky looking
Down on another phase of our earth's
Magnificence.

Our witness to the birth and passing
Of each season renews our faith
In new life...for we are a part of
Our Lord's creation.

NATURE'S TANTRUM

The thundering crash of stormy cymbals
Shatter the quiet of sleep
As slashing streaks of lightening
Tear apart the darkness of night.
Ghostly shadows appear, then vanish
In the magic of light.
Nature's tantrum displays her power
And passes as quickly as it occurred,
Moving on to become a distant rumble
Muffled by the soothing sound of raindrops
Drumming on the rooftop.
Dark skies mirror the awesome sight
Of Spring's first storm
With the promise of new life to follow.
One is slowly lulled to sleep again
By the calm after the storm,
Awakening to a fresh new day
Comforted by the warmth
Of a morning sun.

WHAT A WONDERFUL FALL WE'VE HAD THIS SUMMER

Day after day it's more clouds and rain,
Below normal is the temperature rule.
If you try and dress for the season
You're sure to look like a fool.

The weatherman says he can't help it
And you know that this is a fact.
It's obvious he has no control.
I'm convinced his job is an act.

How nice it would be if sunshine you'd see
With white clouds and blue sky above,
To be able to dress and not second guess
The weatherman's charts that we love.

LATE SUMMER

Dusk comes a little sooner now
And the night air has a welcome coolness.
The quiet of evening captures a symphony
Of sound created by nature's creatures -
Awakened by the dark
And heard only at this time of year.

The moon has a special magic
Touching everyone's heart
As it prepares for the harvest ball,
Lingering in the sky above
Long after the break of day,
Reluctant to leave.

The grass is wet with dew
In the freshness of dawn,
With fragile wisps of fog
Veiling summer's beauty.
And flowers open sleepy eyes
Touched by the morning sun.

The mourning dove's call sounds more plaintive now,
The cardinal's whistle so clear,
As sunlight filters through the haze
And the end of summer draws near.

A SPECIAL DAY

The rising sun shines in a sky of blue
Amidst towering clouds of white
That seem to tumble everywhere
In the early morning light.

Flowers open sleepy eyes
Awakened by a songbird's call,
Then sip the morning dew
And stand up straight and tall.

Feathered splashes of color
Are darting here and there,
Like small colorful kites blown by the wind
On a day that's cool and fair.

A summer's day is dawning
And there is beauty everywhere,
As the earth and sky are joined
In a picture beyond compare.

EARLY SPRING

The tender shoots of young plants shrink
From their cold and frosty cover
As warmth from the rising sun protects
Like a loving, watchful mother.

The birds that flew to warmer climes
When winter came our way,
Are starting to return again
Adding pleasure to each day.

Little clumps of feathers wait
To bathe their colors bright
In the water of the bird bath
That was frozen overnight.

The buds on trees are swelling
As new life stirs within.
The sleeping beauty of nature
Still dozing now and then.

The world is breathing spring,
There's new growth all around -
A gradual change of seasons
With wondrous sights and sound.

The sky above a deeper blue
And clouds a fluffy white -
The cloak of darkness softens
When worn on springtime nights.

NATURE'S CHILD

The Wind, with changing moods, is Nature's impish child.
Sometimes soft and quiet, sometimes rough and wild.
With Sky and Earth for a playground, its behavior knows no bounds.
And being an unruly child, has its repertoire of sounds.

Romping through the flowers, it gently shakes their heads,
Pausing for a moment to gather fragrance from their beds.
Tumbling across the plains and sighing through the trees,
It whispers to the grass of mountains and of seas.

Moving softly as night falls o'er the land,
It touches your cheek with a loving child's hand.
Then reaching out as quietly as can be
It wafts along the beauty of a songbird's melody.

Climbing up into the sky, who could guess its might?
Only gossamer clouds that spread their wings in flight.
Now that we have all been fooled,
Storm clouds touch the earth to show it can't be ruled.

Frolicking in the springtime, before long it becomes tired,
Resting during the summer like any playful child.
Bored with being lazy, it brings Autumn's color show,
Then makes another change to Winter's ice and snow.

The wind that howls with mischievous glee,
Bringing change to Land and Sea,
This imp that drives us wild,
Is not ours – it's Nature's Child.

THE WIND, THE TIDE AND THE SEA

The calmness of the sea
And the fierceness of its roar
With everlasting mystery
Calls you to its shores.
Its nearness somehow
Brings to mind
The peace you've searched
So hard to find.
On its sand life's secrets
Are recorded for a while
And when hidden by the tide
The gods look down and smile.

Two sets of footprints
Far apart
One striding in anger -
One faltering from a broken heart.
There is a sign of hesitancy
In the hurried stride
A quickening of pace in the other
With eagerness hard to hide.
And then they mingle
With obvious joy
The footprints
Of this girl and boy.

Their lovers' quarrel
They cannot hide
And the Sea looks on content...
Their secret life, hidden by the tide.
There are tears and laughter
In the winds from o'er the sea.
Listen to your heart
And choose which yours will be.
For in the sands of time
There is eternity
Where your secret is kept by
The Wind, the Tide and the Sea.

AN UNFORGETTABLE DAY

Soft light defines the separation of Heaven and Earth and shadows
become real as darkness, on runners of wispy fog, slip away pulling a
fragile blanket of mist from the dawning of another day.

The moon's pale, waning light shows through sprays of sunlight splash-
ing against the sky, hiding the wonders of night from view.

A teasing breeze strips gossamer clouds from a clear-blue morning sky
and the sun spotlights summer's beauty.

The bareness of the heavens is gradually covered with fluffy white
clouds reflecting rainbows of color from a setting sun.

Daylight recedes to hide behind a velvet curtain of darkness sprinkled
with diamonds glittering in the moonlight.

Peace settles 'round as the shadows of night softly embrace the moon,
the stars and the sky awaiting the dawning of another day.

To live and see such beauty, if only for a day, leaves a mark upon the
heart time can never take away.

NEW LIFE

The sweetness of a forgotten Spring song
Awakens Mother Earth from her winter slumber,
And she presses the new life of Nature
Against her warm, protective breast.
   The mystery of birth
   The fragrance of life
   The beauty of creation
Are God's gifts to share after a long winter's rest.

To have such beauty for awhile
Stirs Faith within the soul.
I cannot understand why life must end
Nor how new life begins.
   I thank Thee, Lord,
   To possess so much
   Of life and then –
108   Each day die a little, so I too, may live again.

THE FOREST

The forest is a world of beauty
Where Nature rules supreme
Untouched by human frailty
And peace is not a dream.

The intimate warmth of Mother Earth's breast
Releases the fragrance of flowers -
Peeking out from everywhere
Sheltered in Nature's bower.

Silence calms the turbulent mind
And turmoil disappears.
Serenity is found at last.
Life's challenge holds no fears.

The heavens glow with color
Tinged by the setting sun
In its passage to another time and place
Its travels never done.

The quiet of dusk enhances
The soothing murmur of a stream
Flowing through grassy meadows
In this wondrous woodland scene.

Evening shadows form the shroud of night.
The sky is crowned with stars.
Their lustrous beauty bringing
Contentment from afar.

Darkness stirs thoughts of morning
And the joy a new day might bring
Sunshine and flowers, a warm soft shower
The beautiful sound as songbirds sing.

Dawn, pushed by the rising sun,
Gently changes darkness into light.
A new day cleansed with dew is born
Free from the shadows of night.

Visit this gentle wilderness
Untouched by human hands,
An enchanted world that makes hearts light
With peace the soul demands.

AUTUMN'S CROWN

Cornstalks, pumpkins and sheaves of grain
Are a part of nature's show,
With a backdrop of beautiful color
Adding to autumn's glow.

Sunlight on a spider web's dew
Reflects the splendor of fall.
The splashes of color reaching
From earth to tree tops tall.

Harsh winds break the spider's web
And the colors of fall disappear,
As nature paints another scene
For this special time of year.

Falling leaves and barren trees
Against a canvas of brown,
With rainy days and cloudy skies
Are a part of Autumn's Crown.

SEASONS CHANGE

Almost every light in the house is on
Though it's early afternoon.
The sky is gray and rain is falling,
Seems fall has come too soon.

A carpet of golden leaves
Lies 'neath the maple tree.
The glory of fall's beauty
Is such a marvel to see.

The temperature outside mocks the chill
You'd expect to find
On such a dismal day
And the rain one doesn't mind.

The sound of geese in flight
Brings thoughts of winter's clime
And you envy them,
Wishing the sun would shine.

The season's change is always a surprise -
Never quite the same each year
Regardless of their offer,
You enjoy the one that's here.

HURRICANE KATRINA

No one knows who I am
Except me.
Katrina has ravaged my world
And stolen my identity.
I am me,
But there is no one left to know.
Surrounded by death and carnage
There is no place I can go
To find loved ones lost...
Swept away from me
By the fury of Hurricane Katrina
And her raging winds and sea...
Leaving me with nothing
And a terrible fear
Life will never be the same...
Unchanged by my flood of tears
That cannot cleanse the horror of Katrina
And return to me
The world that I once knew...
And my identity.

ABANDONED

Shattered windows, like blackened eyes,
Stare from the face of vacant buildings
Abandoned and left to crumble
Into the dust of forgotten pride.
Entryways stand agape with missing doors,
Unable to hide the decay
And rubble of human neglect.
Weeds and vegetation grow rampant
As though to hide the shame,
All the while adding
To the picture of defeat.
The wind moving from room to room
Deadens the ghostly clamor
Of voices past
Striving to be heard.
But there is no one to listen.
Wrecking balls complete their destruction
And lost forever are the landmarks
That once filled the lives
Of so many with happiness.
Time has once again taken its toll.
Where have the caring ones gone?

HAWAII

When God painted rainbows in the sky
The brush fell from His hand,
Splashing rainbow colors
Throughout this wonderland.

Each island became a rainbow
Their people its pot of gold.
A treasure of love and happiness
For everyone to hold.

The islands are our earthly stars
In a sea of heavenly blue.
More beautiful than the stars above
A paradise come true.

Walk the sands of make-believe
And all your dreams will follow.
Listen to the breeze and surf
As they whisper: "Aloha and Mahalo".

SECTION FOUR:
FAITH

MISSIONARIES

Missionaries…who are they and what is their goal in life?

They are people just like you and me whose dreams of fulfillment and life's work are to share the saving grace of Christ with people in our world who do not know Jesus Christ as their personal Savior.

In doing so, they have accepted the dangers of intrusion into places where Christ is not yet known and accepted. To follow in the footsteps of Christ, they are willing to endure unknown sacrifice for their unselfish love.

In the words of Matthew 28: 19-20, "Go ye, therefore, into all the world and preach the gospel…baptizing them in the name of the Father and of the Son, and of the Holy Spirit…and lo, I am with you always, even unto the end of the world."

God's grace has surely touched you in that you can participate in mission work without enduring the self denial and constant danger existing today in many areas of the world where full-time missionaries have pledged their lives' work in order to share the saving grace of Christ with others. May God's light guide them…and YOU in this love.

There is a treasure for each of us
In the faith we have been given,
A stronger love and understanding…
Adding peace and joy to living.

It only takes <u>one person</u>
To make others aware
There is a God in Heaven
Whose presence is everywhere.

It only takes <u>one moment</u>
To mention His name
And tell them this is why
Our Savior, Jesus, came.

It only takes <u>one prayer</u>
To ask forgiveness of sin
And promise love forever
With faith and hope in Him.

We adore thee and bless thee, Jesus.
By the Holy Cross you have
Redeemed the world.

SAFE JOURNEY

I'd like to leave some footprints
To help others find their way
Down the path that leads to Heaven
Where they might live someday.

I'd like to write a sea of words
On which everyone could sail
That would keep their ship above the waves
And their journey never fail.

I'd like to know that when I've passed
Into God's Holy Realm,
I've helped another on his voyage
To put Jesus at the helm.

I'd like the world to believe
His love can calm life's sea
And bring us closer, closer
Nearer my God to Thee.

GOD'S TREASURE CHEST OF BLESSINGS

To see the glory of His creation,
Hear the beauty of a songbird's melody,
Touch the softness of a rose petal
And smell the fragrance surrounding me.
                For this...I thank you, Lord.

The treasure of God's blessings
We spend each day
With little thought of the wealth
That He has sent our way.
                For this...forgive me, Lord.

Love and happiness, faith and hope
Are gems beyond compare
Given by our heavenly Father
Whose presence is everywhere.
                For this...I love you, Lord.

The blind can see
What others dream might be.
The deaf hear beautiful sound
In the silence of reality.
                For this...they thank you, lord.

The mute have unspoken words
Reflected in their eyes
As they convey with gestures
A spirit that never dies.
                For this...they love you, Lord.

Would you share what you have
With others who have less...
And give to them
God's blessing for happiness?
                For this...God will love you.

THE STRANGER

Small towns are like family
In so many different ways.
Neighbors are close friends
Sharing your life each day.

With a feeling of closeness
No matter how large the crowd,
Everybody seems to belong
And most are honest and proud.

There's always some of course,
That are hard to know.
Families are like this
No matter where you go.

If you should need a helping hand
There are plenty of volunteers.
And should misfortune befall you,
Caring people are always near.

Church provides the bond
That binds everyone together.
Faith in God works wonders
Wherever people gather.

God loves each of us
For we are His family
And when he looks at us
Our love is all He sees.

A stranger came to town one day
And seemed to be alone.
I stopped to welcome him
And make him feel at home.

He had a look about him,
A serenity I've never seen,
And suddenly I wanted to tell him
All about my life and dreams.

I told him about my faith in God,
My blessings, and my family,
And said "I'm searching for life's dream,
To live with God eternally."

THE STRANGER (CONTINUED)

He just smiled and shook my hand,
And as I watched him walk away
It seemed I had always known him
And knew we'd meet again someday.

In a small town of friendly people
A stranger is someone new.
I believe that Jesus walks among us.
Someday He may visit you.

Love thy neighbor as thyself
And to our Savior be true.
Live according to His words,
Life is better when you do.

THE KITCHEN TABLE

The table in your kitchen
Is where each day begins.
On it place the family Bible
And invite our Savior in.

Include Him in your conversation
And take the time to say
You love Him for His blessings
He gives to you each day.

It only takes a moment
And Our Father needs to know
We want Him by our side
Wherever we may go.

The table in your kitchen
Is where good friends gather 'round
Forsaking all the other rooms
For the closeness they have found.

Break bread with Jesus
And all who enter there
In celebration of His love
And ever watchful care.

REMEMBER OUR LORD

The relationship we have with God should never be neglected. Praise Him for His blessings that surround us and assess the wealth that we possess. Foremost are the natural senses given to enjoy His creations. In addition, He has given us Love, Faith, Hope and Happiness.

Material wealth can not bring us closer to our Savior. The acceptance of His word brings us close to Him and at last eternal life in Paradise. This, earthly riches can not buy.

In good times and bad, never forget God. Do you love Him for your wealth? Will you love Him in sickness as you did in health? Will you turn to Him in time of sorrow, asking His help without blame? All this Our Lord must know.

Jesus Christ is the word that holds the promise of life. Never forget Him, and share your blessings with Him. His word will forever be the light to guide us home.

Faith is our most valuable source of wealth. Its worth grows, never losing "trade-in" value and will last forever with the proper care. PRAISE THE LORD!

(Psalms – 106: 1&2) Give thanks to the Lord because He is good. His love is eternal. Who can tell all the great things He has done? Who can praise Him enough?

COME JUST AS YOU ARE

With outstretched arms He waits
For your acceptance of Him
COME JUST AS YOU ARE to worship
And ask forgiveness of sin.

When life's burdens become too heavy
And you stumble along the way
COME JUST AS YOU ARE to Jesus
And bow your head to pray.

Give Him your burden
He will carry it with love.
COME JUST AS YOU ARE and
Walk with Him to Heaven above.

Praise Him for who He is
Our Father and King of Kings.
COME JUST AS YOU ARE to dine
And hear His angels sing.

Love Him as no other
From you He will never part.
COME JUST AS YOU ARE and say:
"Our Father, how great thou art".

MAKE A DIFFERENCE

Make a difference
>Give of yourself to others
Returning God's love for you.
Helping someone in need
Is such a good thing to do.

Make a difference
>God doesn't ask you
To give all you have away.
A little given with love will grow
When returned to you someday.

Make a difference
>This is a challenge...
The Christian way to live...
Love our Savior for his blessings
And ask what you might give.

Make a difference
>Love Jesus every day
And seek what you might do
To show the world he lives,
Helping others less fortunate than you.

Make a difference
>The world awaits your faith.
Be all that you can be
For you alone control the choice
That shapes your destiny.

DEAR LORD, TEACH ME HOW TO PRAY

Where shall I place my body?
How shall I hold my hands?
What words am I to say
That You might understand?
　　　　Dear Lord, teach me how to pray.

In Your name I ask
That You give to me
The strength I need
To forget myself and think of Thee,
　　　　Dear Lord, teach me how to pray.

Is seclusion the answer?
Must I go somewhere alone
To escape my worldly surroundings
And for my sins atone?
　　　　Dear Lord, teach me how to pray.

I need your guidance
To not say me or mine
And love my neighbor as myself
As I partake of bread and wine.
　　　　Dear Lord, teach me how to pray.

Hear my prayers as I think of You
And walk with me each day.
How can I know you?
What must I learn to do and say?
　　　　Dear Lord, teach me how to pray.

THINK ABOUT JESUS

Will you think about Jesus
When you're without need,
Help someone less fortunate
And wish them Godspeed?

This is a challenge given to you,
The Christian way to live.
Love our Savior for his blessings
And ask what you might give.

Returning to God, His love,
Doesn't require riches untold.
Like a shepherd who has lost a lamb
He wants you safe in His fold.

Love Him each day for His blessings
And seek what you might do
To show the world that He still lives,
Helping others less fortunate than you.

FORGIVENESS

Forgiveness is a human need
We often forget to give.
Its power reaches upward
Bringing joy each day we live.

Forgiveness calms a turbulent mind
And soothes an aching heart.
It holds the secret of new life
In which you play a part.

Forgiveness gives up anger
And desire to punish now.
The offense will fade in time.
God's love will show you how.

Tears in the eyes of the forgiven
Wash away the pain of the deed,
And life has more meaning
For the person who's in need.

Let the prayer of forgiveness said by Jesus,
As He was crucified, guide you.
"Please forgive them Father,
126 For they know not what they do."

ROLL AWAY THE STONE

Roll away the stone
That confines your soul.
Free yourself from doubt
Let Heaven be your goal.

Accept our Savior's teaching,
He will lead the way.
As you struggle with temptations
That confront you every day.

Return to Him his love
And feel your spirit soar.
Life on earth is sweeter
As you seek for Heaven's door.

Listen to your heart
When God whispers, "Follow Me".
His footsteps lead to Paradise
Where He wants us all to be.

CATCH THE SPIRIT

Once you feel the love around you
Your life will never be the same.
This feeling is one of wonder
And why our Savior Jesus came.

Rejoice in this blessing
God has given you
And return His live to others
In everything you do.

God's love is contagious
Take it wherever you go.
Life with faith, hope and charity
Brings peace He wants us to know.

Catch the spirit!
Give of yourself to Him.
Hold the hand of Jesus
And ask forgiveness of sin.

THEY SHALL MOUNT UP ON WINGS AS EAGLES

The world was began by Him
Who sits above the earth and sky
And holds cupped in His hands
A place where no one dies.

The Lord is our everlasting God
Who holds all His creation...
The heavens and the stars
And all the earth's nations.

His word endures forever
And He will carry in His arms
Lambs that stray, like a shepherd
And lead His flock away from harm.

Our incomparable God gives strength
To those who trust in the Lord
And turn to Him for help
With faith in His word.

They shall mount up on wings of eagles
And soar to heaven above...
Safe in the arms of Jesus,
With His eternal love.

Based on Isaiah 40:31

THE HOLY TRINITY

GOD THE FATHER

God says "I will always love you".
>   We are born
>   With His love
>   A sacred gift
>   From our Heavenly Father above.

GOD THE SON

Jesus says "I will always be with you".
>   Jesus, Our Savior
>   Opens Heaven's door
>   Teaching God's word
>   He could not offer more.

GOD THE HOLY SPIRIT

The Holy Spirit says "I will give you peace and calm".
>   Believe in Him
>   Live His way
>   Happiness will follow
>   To bless you every day.

THE HOLY TRINITY

"Three divine persons in one"
>   No greater glory
>   Could there be
>   Than sharing live
>   With God for all eternity.

NEVER ALONE

Jesus said "I'll always be with you".
He is forever at your side.
Share you love with Him
And by His Holy Word abide.

There's a joy in knowing
You're never too far from home.
No matter where you wander
You will never be alone.

Life holds untold happiness
Once you have accepted Him.
His strength and love endures
Through all our mortal sins.

Return to God, our Father,
His understanding and love.
Faith will bring you home
To the kingdom of Heaven above.

QUESTIONS

Another birth,
        Another life...
Will there be love?
        Will there be strife?

What earthly gifts await,
        Or are there none?
Only the endless struggle
        Until life's course is run?

Is there really another place
        Where one will always be
Forever loved and happy
        For all eternity?

The Kingdom of Heaven awaits
        Each blessed holy birth.
The gift of life is sacred -
        Loving God will prove its worth.

FAITH IN OUR LORD

When things go wrong
As they sometimes do,
And it seems Our Lord
Has forgotten you,
Remember His love,
It's always there.
Talk to Him
And listen with care.
His Word will guide you
In living each day.
His strength will lift you up
Should you stumble along the way.
Faith in Our Lord
Will help you through
The course in life
He has chosen for you.

GIVING TO JESUS

Give your cares to Jesus.
He will carry them for you.
When you share your life with Him
His light comes shining through.

Give of yourself to His word
And choose Jesus as your friend.
He will never desert you.
His love will never end.

Give Him your hand.
His strength is there for you.
Walk with Him and feel His love
In everything you do.

Give Him your love.
He needs to know you care.
You are part of His family
And your life He wants to share.

AM I WORTHY

God created our world
And the Kingdom of Heaven above,
Jesus gave us His teaching,
The Holy Spirit brought love.

Three Divine Persons in One
Offer life with treasures untold.
His Holy Word can bring
A wealth more precious than gold.

Will my actions honor His memory,
My life reflect his love?
Will He find that I'm unworthy
For the Kingdom of Heaven above?

Hear my prayer Almighty God
And guide me in your ways.
I've never doubted Your Love
But need your strength each day.

IS YOUR FAITH A SECRET?

Closets are a private place
That others seldom see,
Each one concealing who we are
Or what we'd like to be.

Are you a Closet Christian
Hiding your love of Christ from view,
Afraid to tell the world
How much he means to you?

Now is the time to witness to him
And set your life aglow.
Tell your neighbor that He still lives
And help His teaching grow.

Be a disciple of Christ,
Enrich your life with His love,
For all things flow from Him
As you reach for Heaven above.

Don't keep your Christian faith a secret.
Jesus needs you each day.
Prove His death was not in vain
And live your life His way.

SHADOW OF A FRIEND

Shadows are reflections of truth and light
And memories we leave behind.
Yours is one of Christian love,
A very special kind.

Good friends and moments of sharing
Bring life a special glow.
You have given us all of this,
More than you'll ever know.

Your guidance and friendship
Are gifts we treasure
A wealth of caring
Impossible to measure.

May His light shine upon you
And your shadow forever be
A reflection of God's teachings,
FAITH, HOPE and CHARITY.

THE VEIL

How will I know Him
And will he know me?
Will I be welcomed home
As one of His family?

In the face of Jesus the image of God
And the Holy Spirit can be seen.
They are the Holy Trinity of creation,
The guiding light that will forever gleam.

God forgets no one.
His child you'll always be,
Forever welcomed home
And His loving face you'll see.

Blessed are they who witness
To our Heavenly Father's love,
For they shall gain eternal life
In the Kingdom of Heaven above.

The invisible veil that separates
His Holy face from view
Will be lifted, with peace and happiness granted
For all eternity to you.

CONFESSION

I'm sorry that I made You cry
And that I offended Thee.
For just a moment I forgot
Your tears were meant for me.

Your death on Calvary
And removal from the cross
To be entombed and then live again
Brought faith to overcome our loss.

Your love will live forever
And I someday hope to be
At home with you in Heaven
And Your smiling face to see.

WOULDN'T IT BE NICE?

Wouldn't it be nice
To take the time to say,
"Thank you, Jesus,
For Your guidance each day"?

Wouldn't it be nice
To think of Him and ask,
"What can I do
To help you with Your task"?

Wouldn't it be nice
To tell Our Lord you know
His love will follow
Wherever you may go?

Wouldn't it be nice
To live each day with Him
And feel the peace and happiness
Of life without sin?

Wouldn't it be nice
To do all these things
And gain the Kingdom of Heaven
That loving God will bring?

GIVING

How do you spend yourself,
The hours and days given you
Not knowing if they are many
Or only but a few?

Do you draw from this wealth of time
To seek God's way of life
And live according to His Word
Helping others conquer strife?

The selfish person, be he rich or poor,
Gives only that which does not take away
From what he feels he needs
And should be his each day.

Forgotten is the Gift of Life
From our Heavenly Father above.
This precious time is worthless
If we forsake God's love.

We have but one life, one God.
Will your gift to him compare
With two coins of copper,
Given with all the love a heart could bear?

HEAVENLY FATHER

I can not choose your path to follow.
I will only point the way
And promise to be near you
As you live your life each day.

When the gates of Heaven are opened
I will cradle you in My arms
And carry you home to angels
Forever safe from harm.

FAITH AND LOVE

Dear Jesus, I need Your strength
For my faith to endure.
I've never doubted Your love
But now I have to be sure.

How much suffering must I bear?
What more can I give?
These questions might have been Yours
When you wanted so much to live.

The burden of those dear to my heart
Has drenched my soul with tears.
Their cross so heavy, no lighter than mine,
Won't You help us conquer fear?

With faith and love
I open my heart to You
And should I fail, please lift me up
I'll live as You want me to.

THE MEANING OF FAITH

Why do we go to church on Sunday
When we have "so much" to do?
It isn't always to worship God,
There's a selfish feeling, too.

Some of us go because of habit,
Or maybe to wear new clothes.
Others think its "the thing to do"
And make sure that everyone knows.

Some people go 'cause they're lonesome
And don't seem to have many friends.
Church is social gathering
They eagerly wait to attend.

Not everyone goes for obvious gain.
Most want to be with our Lord,
To give thanks for all of their blessings
And return what they can afford.

Whatever the reason you choose to attend,
Deep in your heart you know
Our Lord is there to love you
And that's why you really go.

Remembering Christ on His birth and death
Isn't all that we should do,
To show we believe that He still lives
And recite a prayer or two.

Christmas is a birthday party
A time for love and joy
When God our Father lovingly gave
The world His baby boy.

Easter is a time for sorrow
When his father called Him home.
He died that we might believe in God
And for our sins atone.

THE MEANING OF FAITH (cont.)

God remembers each of us
For we're His children, too.
And if you don't forget Him,
His home has room for you.

LONELINESS

I searched the barren plain of loneliness
To find a sign of love
And in my darkest hour
A light shone from above.
As I raised my eyes toward Heaven
I heard a whisper soft and clear
"Have faith and you will find the strength
To conquer all your fear".

GOD'S LIGHT

There's a star for everyone.
Look up into the sky
And know that yours is there
Waiting to bring a sigh.

Share your dreams
With God's point of light
And climb the stairs of faith
To touch this Holy sight.

Heaven was meant for each of us
The stars and you and I.
His light will shine forever
And life will never die.

REJOICE IN NEW LIFE

Give to me your love
That's all I ask of you
And in return I promise help
In everything you do.

I am your brother, Jesus,
We will never be apart
Forever joined together
Within our Father's heart.

Listen to His Holy word
That I was born to say.
His voice is mine
On this most Holy day.

Rejoice in new life
As heavenly angels sing.
Our Father wishes you
The best that life can bring.

FAMILY

We are brothers and sisters
No matter the color of skin.
Our Heavenly Father has told us
That all human beings are kin.

The world is so large and different,
How could this possibly be?
We are not brothers and sisters
And a part of one family!

God is the Father of all of us
No matter the color of skin
And all Christians know that someday
We'll live together with Him.

A NEW BEGINNING

There's a beautiful gladness
As church bells ring
To herald the presence
Of our Lord and King.

Rejoice as you enter
His house to pray,
Give thanks for the joy
Of living His way.

A new beginning
Is offered by Him,
Forgiveness of transgressions
And freedom from sin.

Follow your heart
And His holy word.
His love will guide you.
Your prayers will be heard.

GOOD MORNING, JESUS

You can never be too close to God.
Share with Him your life each day.
He is the creator of all things
And the blessings that come your way.

Do not shrink away from Him
When days are hard to start
He will grant you peace
And mend a broken heart.

He is always by your side
No matter what you do.
Remember His eternal love
And that Jesus died for you.

Tell our Savior that you know
He is with you every day
And ask that He forgive you
When you forget to say:

"Good morning, Jesus,
I'm so glad that you are here.
We'll spend the day together,
Life's complete when you are near."

GOD WATCHES OVER ME

When I close my eyes I see Jesus
Holding out His hand
To lead me out of darkness
Into the Promised Land.

His love and strength so strong
There is nothing I have to fear.
Heavenly angels sing His praise
I'm so thankful He is near.

When I am fast asleep
God watches over me
And when I awake
His blessings I can see.

Without Him I am nothing.
Life would pass me by.
His love is now and forever...
With Him I shall never die.

SUNDAY OUTING

Let's go to God's House,
There's always someone there,
To let Him know He's in our thoughts
And show Him that we care.

We'll meet His family and His friends,
Exchange a word or two,
And make our "Sunday Outing"
The best thing we could do.

QUESTIONS

How long has it been
Since our Savior's birth?
How long has it been
        Since He was crucified?
How long has it been
        Since He rose from the dead?
How long has it been
        Since He walked by your side?

What have you done
        To remember Jesus?
What will you do
        To return His love?
Have you tried to live
        According to His word?
Will you follow Him
        To Heaven above?

Do you believe
        In Jesus and His Resurrection?
Do you believe
        He died for you?
Do you believe
        In His eternal Love?
Do you believe?
        Show Him you do!

A SMILE

It's awesome what a smile can do.
Almost like magic the sun shines through.

The sky may be cloudy and filled with rain,
A smile warms the heart and eases pain.

A smile is "Hello" and "I love you", too.
A smile hides tears when you say adieu.

A smile will help you through each day.
No words are needed when a smile comes your way.

STEP BY STEP

Step by step, the stairway to Heaven
Is built with Eternal Love.
And the sharing of life's blessings
From our Heavenly Father above.

Live could not offer more
Than sharing it with Him.
What greater glory could there be
Than His forgiveness of sin?

In our journey ever upward
Hold tightly to His hand.
Guardian angels sing His praise
As we step into the Promised Land.

DON'T QUIT – KEEP GOING – YOU'RE DOING FINE!

All things flow from Him above
        Look around you and return His love.
Count your blessings one by one
        And say these words "Thy will be done".
Trust in God and your life will be
        In loving hands for eternity.
Let the faith within your heart
        Bring His love to each day's start.
Try to remember, the world needs you
        And whatever Our Lord wants you to do.
When you're discouraged and full of doubt
        And you wonder what life's all about,
Turn to God and His light will shine.
        Don't quit, keep going, you're doing fine!

A SILENT PRAYER

A mountain top close to Heaven
I saw clearly in my mind,
And knelt in silent prayer
Leaving earthly cares behind.

I praised God for His blessings
And gave my heart to Him,
Feeling love I've never known
As I asked forgiveness of sin.

I could almost feel His touch,
His love was everywhere.
What greater glory could there be?
I knew that He was there.

In the solitude of worship
There is peace beyond compare.
Being close to God brings happiness
And a Father's love to share.

PRAISE GOD

There is an emptiness in our hearts
That only God can fill.
Love Him as no other
And live according to His will.

Drink from the chalice of faith
That He has offered you
And praise Him above all others
For He is lonely too.

Tell Him that you love Him
As you live your life each day
And ask for His forgiveness
If you should lose your way.

JESUS IS FAMILY

God seems so far away
As though He isn't real.
Walk with Christ, for they are one
And His Holy love you'll feel.

Pass through the fires of life
With Jesus by your side
To happiness only faith can bring
And by His Holy word abide.

Jesus Christ is family.
His blood flows through your heart
And when life becomes a burden
From you He'll never part.

The glory of our Heavenly Father
Waits outside life's fiery door.
Jesus Christ is there with love
And life for evermore.

GOD'S HOUSE

The building stood cold and empty
Without warmth or love to share
And though it always beckoned
No one took the time to care.

A cross upon the bell tower
Said this was our Lord's home.
I opened the door and entered
Knowing I was not alone.

As I knelt in silent prayer
A dusty cross on the wall
Reminded me of neglect
And the need to hear His call.

I told Him I was sorry
As His light came from above
And promised our dear Savior
To fill His house with love.

My tears were flowing freely
And I in anguish cried,
"How could Christians let this happen,
Is this why Jesus died?"

Passers-by saw the light
That had been missing for so long,
And one by one they came inside
To praise our Lord in song.

Holding hands they were united
In the presence of God above
For they were all his children
And filled His house with love.

The building now stands warm and full
Of Christians willing to share.
The blessings God has given them
To show Him that they care.

MY NAME IS JESUS

I am Jesus the Son of God
Our Heavenly Father gave me life
To die on Calvary
In atonement for your sins
And from death to set you free.

I am Jesus the Son of God
      My heavy cross and crown of thorns
      My suffering for mortal sin
      Will someday bring you peace
      And eternal life with Him.

I am Jesus the Son of God
      Do not think of me as gone.
      My love will forever stay
      Our Heavenly Father called me home
      Where you might live someday.

I am Jesus the Son of God
      My Holy Spirit is with you
      And I will hold your hand
      To lead you in God's way
      As you try to understand.

I am Jesus the Son of God
      Do not cry for me
      And do not grieve.
      My pain and suffering is done
      In this you must believe.

I am Jesus the Son of God
      Remember my mortal life
      And when I lived with you.
      I was born to teach His word
      And show what you must do.

I am Jesus the Son of God
      I did not know when I would leave
      Or when my work was through.
      I only know that I was blessed
      To live on earth with you.

I am Jesus the Son of God
      Live you life with faith in Him

MY NAME IS JESUS (CONTINUED)

And we will be together again
      Remember my love and crucifixion
      To free the world from sin.

RETURNING GOD'S LOVE

Our Lord has many homes, some more
Beautiful than others, each filled
With His love. Devoted Christians are
the building blocks, their devotion
and love more important than the
structural material. For without
love and sharing of God-given possessions,
His house will crumble.

To build a lighthouse and keep its
beacon burning, so that those who
follow will not become lost, requires
each of us to return to God a portion
of His blessings. To be bathed in His
Holy light and guided to salvation
is a greater reward, by far, than
any earthly prize.

The church is our comfort and
strength, a place from which we
take so much and that asks so little
in return.

GOD'S GLORY

I awakened this morning to the sound
of music sung by a beautiful songbird.

It was preening in all its finery on
the stage of a bush outside my window.

I opened the curtains wide to the glory
of God's creation and marveled at its
performance of one of Nature's compositions.

My songbird flew away leaving behind a
colorful feather as a reminder of its
beauty and God's gentle way of
granting another day.

SEARCH FOR HEAVEN

Please accept what I have done.
The battle of illness I have won.
　　　Do not grieve for me
　　　For I am at last free.
No more pain and wanting love,
Safe in the arms of Our Father above.
　　　Home at last and eternal rest,
　　　This is the end of life's greatest test.
You could not have given me more...
But I chose to open Heaven's door.
　　　My search has ended and I know
　　　Your love will follow wherever I go.

GOD'S LIGHT

The sun has a beautiful light
As it sets at end of day
Casting shadows of nature's wonders
As it journeys on its way.

The heavens glow with color
Painted by God's holy hand...
A picture of peace and beauty
Ever changing at His command.

Our world and its heaven
Belong to only Him.
He is the creator of all things
And His light will never dim.

Bask in the sunshine given you
And as evening shadows fall,
Remember our Savior is waiting
For your faithful, loving call.

FATHERS' DAY

Happy Fathers' Day, Dear God,
Creator of our world.
We shall forever keep
The flag of faith unfurled.

Heavenly Father, we thank you
For your watchful care each day,
And for our mortal Dads,
A special love we pray.

On this special day for fathers,
How happy You must be,
To have your son beside you,
As our world you oversee.

FAMILY LOVE

God the Father...
God the Son...
God the Holy Spirit...
Three divine persons in one.

They are the Holy Trinity
That gives life its love,
With everlasting faith
In our heavenly Father above.

God gave the gift of love.
No greater love could be.
Live according to His word
And His Holy Face you'll see.

We are His family,
Born to be with Him.
Listen to His words
And seek forgiveness of sin.

THE JOURNEY

If you travel the Path
That leads to God,
Faith will guide you each day.
No matter how long the journey,
The kingdom of Heaven's
A heartbeat away.

THANK YOU, JESUS

Church is my light...
Its family God's love,
Reaching out to brothers and sisters
As commanded by Him above.

God has many homes on earth,
As he has in Heaven above.
Each one a haven for Christians
Seeking His eternal love.

Love His son, Jesus, as no other
For there will never be
Another willing to be crucified
For our sins to set us free.

Thank you, Jesus, for your love...
Father and Son are one.
We pray to the Holy Spirit,
Thy will be always done.

GOD'S LOVE

Beyond the horizon that we see
Is a world where we will always be.
A place our Heavenly Father created
With love for you and me.

Don't worry about the day
When our Heavenly Father will come.
He will lead you safely home,
Forgiving transgressions you may have done.

Praise the Lord with song, play music
And shout for joy to the Lord, our King.
He is faithful to His promises
When love and service we bring.

By His own power and strength, He rules.
He has won the victory
And will judge with justice fair and good
His people throughout eternity.

DISCIPLE'S BLESSED DESTINY

The way you hold my heart
To help me understand,
With my very soul
In the palm of Your hands.
This is my blessed destiny.

To face the challenge
That you have given me,
I need your strength.
You are the Father, I am family.
This is my blessed destiny.

Give me hope and faith.
Your wish is my command.
Fill me with trust and love
As in your light I stand.
This is my blessed destiny.

Let my words speak
Of your wonderful ways
Telling all those I meet
To thank you every day.
This is my blessed destiny.

FOR ALL WHO BELIEVE

Jesus, our Savior, the Son of God,
Was born like you and me.
Not a part of imagination
But someone we could see.

He lived, our Savior lived,
Teaching His Holy words,
The unseen Spirit of God
With words no one had heard.

He taught salvation and eternal life
For all who would follow Him
Into the Kingdom of Heaven
Free at last from mortal sin.

And then one day, His mission done,
Our Father called Him home.
He was crucified to show
That He was not alone.

For all who believe in him
His death was not in vain.
Practice your faith in God
And love His holy name.

PRAYER OF THANKS

Heavenly Father, give us the strength and guidance to walk in Your light.
Save us from becoming lost in the shadows.

We pray for forgiveness of our transgressions that may have offended thee and offer our thanks for the happiness found in living life each day with You.

As we share this season of harvest, we thank you for our many blessings grown in the field of faith from a seed of love planted and nurtured by so many.

We ask your help with new plantings so that the field for faith will not lay fallow and we can see your teachings grow.

We thank You for Your love, enough for everyone to carry and scatter along the way, leaving a path to follow.

AMEN

WHAT DID YOU DO?

What did you do today, my friend?
What did you do today?
Did you take the time to thank our Lord
For helping you on your way?

What will you do tomorrow, my friend?
What will you do tomorrow?
Will you learn from what you did today
And leave no time for sorrow?

What did you do yesterday, my friend?
What did you do yesterday?
It's never to late to make amends.
It's never too late to pray.

COMMITMENT TO FAITH

Why do I support my church?
Is there more that I could do?
These are questions we all should ask.
We need our Lord and He needs you.

Our lives are enriched because of His words
And we should share His needs.
The blessings God has given us
We can never repay in deeds.

Church is a place where Christians gather,
A temple for God's love,
Where all who seek salvation
Find faith in Him above.

Church fills a void in our lives,
Prayers ease the pain of strife,
As you open your heart in acceptance
Of Him that gave you life.

Commitment builds a house for our Lord
With gifts from both young and old.
Join with them to make a place
Where His life's story is told.

DOES IT RAIN IN HEAVEN?

Does it rain in Heaven
And does it get cold?
These are things I wonder about
Because someday I'll be old.

My Grandma and my Papa
Don't like the rain and snow.
They need warm days and sunshine.
I just have to know.

Someday they'll live there.
Our minister said so,
And if this is where they are
That's where I want to go.

My Mom and Dad said, "No problem,
'Cause that's where we'll all be
And do everything together
With friends and family".

I think there's kids in Heaven
That didn't mind the rain and snow.
I just wondered about getting old
And living there, you know.

I hope you'll help me, God,
With what I ask of you,
Because you are my best friend.
Who else can I turn to?

THE HOLY SACRAMENT OF BAPTISM

The Holy Sacrament of Baptism
Was being given to one of God's newest angels,
As yet untouched by human frailty...
And not too far from the arms of our Heavenly Father.

The baby looked out at the world
With a beautiful angelic smile
While being cradled in the arms of our pastor.

At the moment of baptism what special vision
Was seen to bring forth such awesome beauty?
This sacred moment was a bonding of Father and child...
With a promise of eternal love.
It was a joy to behold.

GOD LOVES YOU

You are a child of God.
Carry yourself with pride.
Walk with head held high
And by His word abide.

Hold the hand of Our Father
As you walk with Him each day.
Look up to God with love
And stride through life His way.

Be willing to tell the world
Your heart belongs to Him
And be unashamed to ask
For His forgiveness of sin.

Visit God in church.
He is always there.
Share with Him His blessings
He needs to know you care.

Don't stay away too long
For God has heartaches, too.
Share with Him life's burdens.
He will carry them for you.

A STAR FOR EVERYONE

There's a star in Heaven for everyone.
A light of love to lead you home,
When your earthly task is done.

What joy to live in the Lord's earthly realm,
Sailing the sea of life with him at the helm.
Have faith and your destiny
Will be paradise for eternity.

Do not despair when storms are met.
He will help with the course you've set.
His word can calm the troubled sea,
And bring your life tranquility.

Oh, Sweet Jesus, abide with me,
While I sail life's troubled sea.
Keep me safe where ever I roam,
So that I may find my way back home.

A VALENTINE FOR EVERYONE

Remember your first valentine
And the joy you knew
In receiving a card with words
That were meant for only you.

You're never too young for a sweetheart
Or a friend to share life's love.
How blessed we are to have them...
Our valentine from above.

You're never too old for a valentine
And the love God meant you to know.
Share your feelings with someone
Give life a special glow.

There's a valentine for everyone
Way up there in the sky.
A heart so big, it holds the world
With room for you and I.

Every day is Valentine's Day
For our Heavenly Father above.
His words will bring salvation
There is no greater love.

Give Him a valentine in return.
It takes only a moment or two
And say, "The world's a better place
Because of love from you."

LOVE YOUR NEIGHBOR AS YOURSELF

When you give of yourself to others
You are returning God's love for you.
Helping someone in need
Is such a good thing to do.

The sharing of God's blessings,
To give someone a better day,
Leaves a warm feeling in your heart
In a very special way.

Telling your friends about Jesus
And the love he has for them
Is just being a good neighbor
As you share your love for him.

God doesn't ask you to give
All that you have away.
A little given with love will grow
When returned to you someday.

Love our Heavenly Father
As Jesus taught us to do.
What a wonderful way to live
With the promise of Heaven for you.

PREPARATION

We're going on vacation...
Gonna take a long awaited trip,
The kids have even worked part time
And put away their tips.

We've saved everything we could,
Cut corners here and there,
And carefully chosen the roads to take
With things we all could share.

We're leaving next Sunday.
Can't wait to get away.
Wish we had another week
But can't afford to stay.

I know we'll have a good time.
We've planned this trip for years.
The Good Lord owes us this
For all our sweat and tears.

Our vacation was everything we planned
And we're back home safe and sound,
With thoughts of church and Jesus
And the pleasures we had found.

All of us went to God's house.
We knew that He was there
As we humbly bowed our heads
And offered Him our prayers.

The trip that we had taken
Could very well be our last,
For living costs so much
And time goes by so fast.

But wait...there's another trip
That no one can escape.
The destination is the same.
What planning will it take?

PREPARATION (Cont.)

Open your heart to Jesus
And all his blessings share.
The kingdom of heaven awaits
For those who show they care.

Follow the path that leads to God.
Faith will guide your feet each day.
No matter how long the journey,
The destination's a heartbeat away.

FIRST COMMUNION

As you receive the body and blood
Of our Savior, Jesus Christ,
You are given life's greatest treasure.
　　　Not toys or clothes
　　　Or everyday desires…
　　　But love beyond measure.
You are a child of God…
And a part of Him.
Blessed are God's children
Who seek forgiveness of sin.
　　　May the joy of First Communion
　　　Continue your whole life through,
　　　And your love of God grow stronger…
　　　As you keep Him close to you.

LOVING JESUS

He who loves the Lord
Is richer by far
Than the wealthiest of men
Who have never seen his star.

Love him with the same love
That he has given you,
And you will feel his presence
In everything you do.

He is our Savior and King.
There is no sacrifice in loving him.
He holds the promise of eternal life
For forgiveness of mortal sin.

Follow his guiding light
As you live your life each day
And hand in hand you'll enter Heaven
Where we were born to stay.

VEIL OF LOVE

Follow the light of our awesome God
As you sail life's turbulent sea.
He will guide you safely home
To Heaven's shores and tranquility.

Heaven awaits all God's children
And we will someday be
At home with loved ones
For all eternity.

The veil that separates
God's holy face from view
Disappears with His embrace...
And the words, "My child, I love you."

GOD'S LIGHT

In the transition from daylight to darkness, as we enter
The twilight zone, the setting sun touches the horizon...
Splashing a display of beautiful color until it drops from view
To rise again in an unseen world beyond the place where
Heaven and Earth are joined.
Leaving behind a silence of reverence by all of God's creation
Until the shadow of darkness appears...and their nocturnal
Celebration begins...in the soft light of heaven's glow
Beneath the moon and stars.

O LORD, TAKE MY HAND

You are on my mind
Every minute of every day,
As I strive to hear your words
That I may learn and teach your way.

O Lord, take my hand
And let me walk with you.
I need you in my life today
And in everything I do.

Let me be a shepherd
And have a flock of my own...
To lead them to green pastures
And peace with you at home.

GIFT OF LIFE

The gift of life is fragile
And wrapped with love
By our Heavenly Father
In the kingdom of heaven above.

Open this gift with praise.
Place the wrappings with care
Where you can touch them...
Knowing He is there.

Cherish this gift of life
That God has given you
And open your heart to Him
In everything you do.

JESUS AND ME

O Lord, in so many ways
You have touched my heart.
Let me share this love
That makes each day a joy to start.

I want to give the world
All you have given me...
A love beyond compare
That will set their spirits free.

The burdens of my life are lifted
As you carry them for me.
I want to walk beside you
And your holy face to see.

PRAYER FOR PEACE

Almighty God and awesome King
Of all nations, we humbly
Pray for peace. Hear our prayers
To Thee.
Let not the blood of your
Creation ebb away into the sands
Of warring nations
Needing Thee.
Help us to love one another
And live as sister and brother
With Thee
Grant us your salvation and
Lead us not into temptation
Forsaking Thee.
May our sins offending
Be forgiven and our love never
Ending be of Thee

Amen

HAPPY NEW YEAR TO THE WORLD

Father God has once again
Sired another year.
May its birth, yet untarnished,
Bring joy and life without fear.

As the world joins in celebration
Of this gift from God above,
Let them join hands as family
And praise His holy love.

Someday we will all be together...
No matter our creed or skin,
For we are His family, brothers and sisters,
Born to live forever with Him.

Rejoice in the New Year,
And pray that peace will reign
Throughout the world...
Bringing hope to His people again.

HAPPY NEW YEAR TO THE WORLD!

BENEDICTION

Jesus said, "I will always be with you..."
I am your brother
And we will never be apart...
Forever we're joined together
Within our Father's heart.
Catch the spirit and never forget
We are as one with the body of Christ
For he is with us yet.
As you leave this holy place today,
Promise to make a difference
And give of yourself to others...
Returning God's love for you.
Be all that you can be...
In Christ's name. Amen

LIFE'S STORY

For every year that passes
A brand new year is born
And from the Book of Life
Another page is torn.

Review what's written on every page
Before it's thrown away.
The words recorded there
Reveal your life each day.

Will you see a kindly spoken word
Or an unselfish caring deed
Given with love to someone
In answer to their need?

Does your life reflect God's teaching?
Do you spend some time with Him?
Will the next page tell a story
You would like to read again?

CROSSROADS

Crossroads is a place on the highway
Of life that God ordained should be...
A choice in direction and a path
To set our spirits free.

Crossroads is a place that holds the joy
Of sharing life with Him
And the blessings of His creation
As we seek forgiveness of sin.

Crossroads is a place of Christian love
Where our church will someday be...
The pathway to new life in heaven
For all eternity.

The seeds of faith, hope and love
Sown in this holy place
Reap a harvest of His promise
To someday see His holy face.

SAFE HARBOR

Heaven is a safe harbor
Sheltered from life's tides
With shores untouched by sadness
Where happiness and peace abide.

It's beauty is God's creation
With heavenly skies of blue
And waters reflecting your image
With Jesus beside you.

A place that holds the joy
Of eternal life with Him
The paradise He promised
Free from earthly sin.

Heaven awaits all God's children
And we will someday be
At home with loved ones
For all eternity.

Follow the light of our awesome God
As you sail life's turbulent sea.
He will guide you safely home
To heaven's shores and tranquility

The veil that separates
God's holy face from view
Disappears with His embrace
And the words, "My child I love you."

PASTOR AND SHEPHERD
DR. EARL OWEN – 1996

Was there a voice you heard
That made you choose
Or was there no voice at all
To make you walk in shepherd's shoes?

The path you chose
Has been walked before
By other shepherds and their flocks
To pastures beyond Heaven's door.

Each lamb that strays
From God's chosen trail
A shepherd tries to rescue
So their journey doesn't fail.

Through deep valleys and shadows,
Prayers help find the way.
Though the upward trail be steep
A shepherd leads each day.

You have been our shepherd.
We'll miss you when you leave.
You've been His chosen one.
You taught us to believe.

As you lay down your staff,
Choirs of angels will sing,
We join them in wishing you
The best that life can bring.

YOUR CHURCH-YOUR HERITAGE

Portage First is a church of God
Created by Christian souls...
A temple of His wondrous love
Where heaven is our goal.

Inside these holy walls
Live memories of long ago...
Families and friends built a refuge
That anyone could know.

In the quiet of meditation,
As you bow your head in prayer
Giving thanks for all those brave, good folks.
There's a feeling that they are there.

From horseback circuit rider
To the pastor we now know,
Our past and present mingle
In the light of heaven's glow.

The words of God haven't altered.
We are still His family,
Born to live with Him each day
Throughout the centuries.

Our heritage we cherish
And will keep striving every day
Pledging that those who follow
Have a church where they can pray.

WHERE WILL YOU MEET HIM?

When you're in the hands of God
There's no better place to be.
His love will give salvation
On Earth and for eternity.

As you stand upon the mountain top
Give thanks with praise and prayer
To our dear Lord in heaven
For His blessing that brought you there.

Remember the dark, deep valleys
When our Savior held your hand....
To lead you ever upward
And help you understand.

Our Lord can lift you up
And once more make you whole
When mortal pain and suffering
Has taken its earthly toll.

He is in the valleys
And on the mountain top above
Reaching out to each of us
With His eternal love.

Where will you meet Him
As you seek to live his way?
He is always all around you
And is with you every day.

GOD'S LOVE

When I think about love,
I think about God and all He's given me.
I count His blessings, one by one
And even those I cannot see.

There are times I must admit,
I have forsaken Him
And for this I ask forgiveness
Of my transgressions and sin.

His strength is all around me...
No burden too heavy to share.
He will carry you in His arms
If you turn to Him in prayer.

Although God, our Heavenly Father, gives
He also takes away
And we try to understand
As we bow our heads and pray.

We are all of us God's children
And someday we will be
At home with our Heavenly Father
For all eternity.

WALK TO EMMAUS

Welcome to a three day journey
That will change your life.
In the silence of acceptance
Praise Him…and forget all earthly strife

God seems so far away
As though He isn't real.
Walk with Jesus for they are one
And His holy love you'll feel.

This is the first step.
Give yourself completely to Him.
Make your world His
And ask forgiveness of sin.

His love will ease the burden
That weighs you down each day.
His strength will lift you up
As you search to live His way.

The three day Walk to Emmaus…
With our Loving Savior near
Will make your burden lighter
As you share heartache and tears.

Hold the hand of your new found friend
As you complete the circle of love,
And raise your voice in praise and song
To our dear Savior above.

May the communion and burdens shared
Bring you the peace you seek,
For God's glory is given
To the humble and the meek.

Day Four will follow
Your whole life through,
With your Walk to Emmaus a pattern…
The Kingdom of Heaven waits for you.

WALK TO EMMAUS – DAY ONE

There is no silence
Where His voice cannot be heard.
There is no sound more glorious
Than our Savior's loving words.

In the solitude of meditation
And the worship of our Savior and King,
Thee is no greater joy
Than loving Him can bring.

Follow His guiding light
Your whole life through.
Let His love touch your heart
In everything you do.

On this first day feel His presence and know that He will never let
you carry life's burdens alone. Give your burden to Him as of now.
He is waiting...for you are His child. His love surrounds you!

SECTION FIVE:
FUNERALS

ETERNALLY YOURS

There is a place for you and me
That we will share eternally,
Never again to be apart;
My partner in life,
My angel sweetheart.

I go to prepare a place for you,
So you won't be alone.
Where we can be together,
In the paradise of God's home.

MY WISH

Let not the darkness of the grave
Deny my wish for light...
For I have returned to God
With everlasting sight.

Cast my ashes in the wind
Where rains can touch my cheek
And sunshine warm my heart
As I hear angels speak.

Let me wander with the wind
To be carried into the sky
And catch a glimpse of Heaven
Where I shall never die.

When soft winds touch your face
You will know that I am near...
Still watching over you,
For I'll always love you, Dear.

REST QUIETLY, MY LOVE

I will not mourn
For you will always be
Within my heart and memory.

I cannot cry,
Nor will I grieve,
For you have found true happiness.
In this, I do believe

Till we're together again,
Never more to part,
Rest quietly, my love,
You'll always have my heart.

I'LL WAIT FOR YOU

I'll wait for you at the gates of Heaven
Where we'll start our lives anew.
For Heaven would be lacking,
After living on earth with you.

I believe in God, the Father Almighty,
And all His words so true.
But the Kingdom of Heaven will have to wait,
Till I enter it with you.

GOD'S LOVE

Death is only a heartache to the living
For they know not what it holds
Everlasting life is the promise of Jesus
In the sweetest story ever told.

Release yourself from your sorrow
Have faith and you will be
At home again with loved ones
For all eternity.

Our heavenly Father would never separate you
Or take away your love.
He wants you together with Him
In the kingdom of Heaven above.

DEAR HEART

We never said goodbye
As you quietly slipped away
With our Dear Savior Jesus –
What could we really say?

You were going home
To prepare a place for me
Where we will be together
For all eternity.

We will never be separated
Even though we are apart
Until I join you in Heaven
Rest quietly, Dear Heart.

We'll be together again.
This I believe is true.
My life will be complete
In Paradise with you.

HEAVEN IS HOME

Heaven is home
And we all can return someday.
No matter our earthly journey.
God's love will light the way.

Eternal life is granted
To all who enter there...
Free from mortal suffering
Safe in our Father's care.

And so friend, do not grieve
For the one who has gone away.
They have found the happiness
You will also know someday.

Praise God for His blessings.
He hasn't deserted you.
Hold tightly to His hand.
His love will see you through.

LONELINESS

It's when you go to bed at night,
Turn the covers down
And touch the presence no longer there
Dressed in her night-time gown.

It's everything that you shared...
Every moment of every day
And life will never be the same
Now that she has gone away.

And yet she is never very far.
God would not have it so,
For she has left a love
That follows wherever you may go.

Thank you, my darling,
For my precious memories
And a love beyond compare
That you have given me.

BACK HOME

Everyone goes back home again,
This is God's promise true
Heaven is back home
And He's waiting there for you.

Angels brought us to this earth
Cradled in loving arms
And when life is over
Take us back home safe from harm.

Loved ones that have gone back home
Are waiting there for you.
Surrounded by God's Holy Love
You'll live a life that's new.

The joy of reunion back home,
With those who went away,
Is everything our Father promised
That we would know someday.

No matter how long our earthly life
We were never meant to stay.
A better life awaits back home,
Because Jesus came our way.

SEPARATION

I didn't tell you often enough
How much you mean to me.
Who really ever thinks
That life will not always be?

Separation is hard to bear.
Tears can't wash away the pain.
My heart will always ache,
Until we meet again.

We'll be together someday,
With family and friends,
Never to part again
In a life that never ends.

COME HOME

When I was a child
And went outside to play
My father's loving voice
Called me home at end of day.

In fading light he held me
Close in his caring arms.
I was so glad to be there,
Loved and safe from harm.

In the twilight of life
I remember back then, and
Hear our Heavenly Father's voice
Calling me home to be with Him.

Once again I will hurry home
To a Father's love -
Surrounded by family and friends
In the Kingdom of Heaven above.

HEAVEN ISN'T VERY FAR

Heaven isn't very far.
In a heartbeat you are there
As an angel holds your hand
With tender loving care.

No one ever dies.
They are just away
And though you cannot see them
Are with you every day.

They have eternal life with Jesus
In the paradise of God's home
With family and friends around them
Forever loved and never alone.

There is no heartache or pain, -
No earthly sadness or tears
With the arms of God around them
There is nothing they have to fear.

Heaven isn't very far.
Loved ones are always near.
Rejoice in their happiness
God chose them to be there.

NEVER ALONE AGAIN

In my grief I need someone to talk to
But no one has the time.
I only ask they listen and share
A love that once was mine.

Most everyone says, "Call me
No matter when, Dear Friend,"
But no one visits or calls me
To help my broken heart to mend.

I know their lives are busy
And I probably wish for too much,
But God has claimed my angel
With His loving Father's touch.

I only ask that God
Will someday lead me home...
To once again be with my love
And I will never be alone.

THE GOOD FIGHT

He fought the good fight
His battle now is done
No more rounds remain
The game of life he's won.

God took our fighting champ
To live in Heaven above
And never face another challenge
Safe in the arms of love.

He will be filled with happiness
No more pain and tears.
We're thankful that we had him
His strength beyond his years.

SOLITUDE

The solitude of living alone
After a lifetime of growing old
Weighs heavily on your mind
As our Savior you gently scold.

With so many questions unanswered
About living day to day.
What does the future hold?
You have taken my love away.

Why must we be separated?
What purpose could that serve?
After so many years together
There's more that I deserve!

We will meet again someday
Never more to part.
Until then our heavenly Father,
My love will have my heart.

HEAVEN WAITS

I kiss the picture of the face
That one adorned the pillow next to mine,
Giving thanks to God for our love…
Saying, "Heavenly Father, my soul is thine."

Separation is so hard to bear.
My angel was never meant to stay.
She did all you asked…
Keeping you close each day.

Someday we will be together…
A reunion of family,
In Heaven with you, our Father,
Where we were born to be.

FROM SARAH

What a surprise! I had no idea
My earthly life was through.
With all the trips we've made together,
This one I had to take without you.

We never said "goodbye"
As I quietly slipped away
With our dear Savior, Jesus.
What could we really say?

I am now at peace forever.
The angel of death has set me free.
I am safely home in Heaven.
No more pain and grief I'll see.

Jesus himself came to greet me
On that road so hard to trod...
And with his arm to lean on,
I knew I would see God.

Do not grieve for me, dear husband,
For I surely love you still.
Look beyond the shadow of death
And trust our Father's will.

You still have things to do there,
So remember to do them now
According to God's plan for you.
He will show you how.

When your life's work is over
He will also carry you home.
Oh! The wonder of that meeting
And the joy to see you come.

> Eternally yours,
> Your loving wife

GOD'S HAVEN OF REST

Home from the stress of living on Earth,
Safe in God's haven of rest.
What a joy to know such heavenly peace.
This is life at its best.

The hands of time no longer move,
Eternal life you've gained,
With family and friends in Paradise,
Free from heartache and pain.

The teachings of Jesus weren't easy to follow,
Though His directions were always so clear.
You knew by His word and example,
There was nothing that you had to fear.

Faith in God and returning His love
Are all that you're asked to do.
What a wonderful way to live your life
With the promise of Heaven for you.

HE GAVE US LOVE

You took him away too soon, Lord,
Was there really such a need?
He was with us such a short time,
The flower hadn't yet outgrown the seed.

Will you tell him your plans, Lord,
So that he won't be afraid?
He's still a little boy,
Wondering about the change you've made.

Put your arms around him, Lord,
And hold him close each day,
While you tell him about Heaven
Where he will always stay.

Keep him safe, dear Lord,
Until we make our home with You.
Let him know he's not forgotten
And is a part of everything we do.

He will live forever in our hearts, Lord,
You didn't completely take him away.
We thank you for our time with him,
He gave us love each day.

HOLD THE HAND OF JESUS

When your heart is heavy
And filled with pain
Turn to Christ for solace
He will grant you peace again.

To ease the hurt of parting
From a loved one God called home
Hold the hand of Jesus
And you will never be alone.

He will give you strength
And His light guide the way
In acceptance of God's will
As you live your life each day.

Do not forsake our Savior
His words will all come true
No one really ever dies
They are just away from you.

Believe in our Heavenly Father
And you will someday be
With family and friends in Paradise
For all eternity.

MY JOURNEY

The doors of Heaven opened
And I was invited in
For I had been forgiven
Of any Earthly sin.

My journey was a happy one.
I wanted at last to be
At home again in Heaven
And all our loved ones see.

When you walk with Jesus
His light is everywhere.
You'll never lose your way.
His Hand is always there.

Walk with Him, talk with Him -
Faith can show you how.
You will never be alone.
He is with you now.

All life returns to whence it came.
God wants us there with Him
And the hands of time, never still
Bring forth new life again.

I'll wait for you with Jesus
In the wonder of God's Home.
It really isn't very far
And I am not alone.

ETERNAL LOVE

Do not think of me as gone
My love will forever stay.
Our Heavenly Father called me home
Where we will all live someday.

I am with you now
And will always hold your hand.
You'll never be alone
As you try to understand.

Do not cry for me
And do not grieve.
My pain and suffering are done
In this you must believe.

Remember our times together
And the happiness we knew.
Don't let tears wash away
The love God has for you.

I did not know when I would leave,
Or when my work was through.
I only know that I was blessed
To live on earth with you.

DEATH IS ONLY AN INTERVAL

Sleep peacefully, dear one.
Good night and happy rest.
There is nothing in Heaven to fear.
You've passed life's greatest test.

When you awake in Paradise
God will be waiting there.
He was present when you were born.
You have never left His care.

The veil that separated
God's holy face from view
Disappears with His embrace
And the words "My child, I love you".

Though you are gone
You have never left me.
Everything I see and touch
Is a loving memory.

Our house is an earthly one.
Its building blocks, God's love
Blessed by His holy grace...
Another waits in Heaven above.

You have left for a little while
To wait in that house for me...
Beyond the horizon are beautiful tomorrows
We'll share for eternity.

A place of peace and happiness
We can forever call our own.
God's gift for loving Him.
Always together...never alone.

Happy rest with Jesus.
Father and Son are one.
The Holy Spirit brings us peace.
At last God's will is done.

NICOLE

We lost a bit of sunshine
Now that Nicole has gone away
But the light of this free spirit
Will help us find our way.

Pressed between the pages of memories
Are beautiful fragments of love.
The touch and feel of happiness
That's waiting in heaven above.

Let the laughter we once shared
Banish every lonely tear
And believe with all our hearts
That she is always here.

Remember the good times
And enjoy each day with them.
Rejoice in our loved one's happiness
Until we're together again.

There is an emptiness in our hearts
That only God can fill.
Let Him share your grief
And live according to His will.

Heaven isn't very far…
Loved ones are always near.
Rejoice in their happiness.
God chose them to be there.

SWEET SPIRIT

I waited for you to be born
With a heart full of love.
You were my sweet spirit...
God's gift from Heaven above,

And now our Lord has claimed
What He once gave to me.
He couldn't love you more than I
For that could never be.

You were 30 years young -
With so many years to live.
You made my life a joy
With all you had to give.

In my prayers I'll hold your hand
And walk with you each day.
The Lord will keep you safe, sweet spirit,
Every moment you're away.

A part of my heart will be missing
Until we're together again.
Why couldn't I go first?
Oh, how I'll miss you 'til then.

I loved you more than life itself
And now must wait my time
To join you in Heaven
Where forever you'll be mine.

HOME AT LAST

The Angel of Death entered my life
And being so loving and kind,
Let me wander down memory lane
With loved ones in my fast fading mind.

Those who had gone before were happy
And I rejoiced to see them,
For I was coming home
At last...together with Him.

As the Angel of Death
Held open Heaven's door...
Please, one more earthly favor
I humbly implore!

Surrounded by family and friends,
I want to thank all I've ever known
For their Christian deeds
And the love they've shown.

And now I guess it's time
For our Heavenly Father's embrace,
To enter the Kingdom of Heaven
And see His holy face.

Home at last with my guardian angel,
Safe in our Father's arms
Where we will someday be united
Forever happy, free from harm.

Forever love,

SECTION **SIX:**
WEDDINGS/
ANNIVERSARIES

CHALICE OF LOVE

Wedding anniversaries are a celebration
Of marriage vows once made.
Romantic memories of promise
That time will never fade.

Each anniversary's a chalice
Filled to the brim with love…
A gift to sweethearts wed
In the presence of God above.

Sip from this cup of love
And together you'll always be
Side by side as promised
For all eternity.

HAPPY LOVE

Another year is ours.
One more page in the book of time.
We've shared sunshine and starlight,
Precious moments that were yours and mine.

I can't remember all our years,
But those I do recall
Were filled with happiness…
Each one the best of all.

As we turn the pages,
Our life unfolds
With all the love
Our hearts can hold

Happy Anniversary, my darling.

OUR WEDDING PRAYER

Our Father which art in Heaven –
We thank you for your love that gave us
The happiness we both share.

Hallowed be Thy name –
We promise to keep this love forever
In our hearts.

Thy Kingdom come, Thy will be done, on earth
As it is in Heaven –
We shall live according to Your word
With faith and trust.

Give us this day our daily bread –
We pray your blessing will follow us
All the days of our lives.

And forgive us our trespasses, as we forgive
Those who trespass against us –
We ask Your guidance in living
And strength to judge not, one another.

Lead us not into temptation, but deliver us from evil –
We will strive to overcome the temptations of
Life that may offend Thee and hand in hand, will follow
Your light to everlasting love as Husband and Wife.

For Thine is the Kingdom and the power and the glory,
Forever and ever –
We stand before You united as one, our happiness
Knows no bounds. Love will keep us together
In this new life we have found.

DADDY'S GIRL

"Daddy's Girl" you will always be,
So how can I "give" you away?
I never thought about the marriage
That would happen someday.

Where have they gone…
Those wonderful precious years
When it seemed you were mine alone
As we shared laughter and tears?

Now that you are grown
And have found another to share
A portion of the love we knew,
I wish you happiness beyond compare.

"Daddy's Girl" you will always be
And hold my heart in your baby hands
As you stand with your chosen one
In answer to God's holy command.

May your future hold the love and happiness you have given me.

Forever love…Dad

TOGETHER

Wedding Anniversaries are like love letters -
Each one cherished in your heart.
Filled with dreams and happy memories
From which you'll never part.

The past is a treasure of love
For husband and wife to share
Life's riches are within each other -
A wealth beyond compare.

Giving your heart to another
In exchange for a love of your own
Is the happiness you've longed for -
A caring you've never known.

If there is no feeling of love
Nothing to bring a sigh
Life is without meaning
And the spirit will wither and die.

Love makes a wedding anniversary
Seem like only yesterday
As time returns to lovers
The joy of their wedding day.

Never forget you are sweethearts
And together you'll always be
Each one telling the other
"I'm so glad you married me!"

TOGETHER AT LAST

Today is the beginning of forever
As wedding bells ring their joyous sound
In celebration of our marriage
And the happiness we have found.

God chose us to love one another.
Together we'll always be
Holding each other close
As we sail life's stormy seas.

The fantasy of sweethearts
Has at last come true.
We're so happy to be married
And share this dream with you.

Family and friends now gathered
Bless us with their love.
You've added to our happiness
And we thank Our Lord above.

A TOAST TO LOVE

It really doesn't matter
How or where,
A boy and a girl in love decide
Each other's life to share.

Perhaps a glance or touch
Released the love inside,
Spilling over with feelings
They could no longer hide.

They're together at last
And stand before us now,
Promising each other eternal love
As they make their marriage vow.

A toast to lovers
Now joined as one:
"May they always cherish
The heart they've won".

SILVER ANNIVERSARY

As we celebrate our wedding vows
Love blends every moment of time.
Yesterday, today and tomorrow
I am yours and you are mine.

No need to count the seasons,
The sunsets or dawn of another day.
Time is lost in the love
That God has sent our way.

Happy Anniversary Sweetheart
As our happiness we share.
Our wedding day was special
Because Darling, God was there.

GOLDEN WEDDING ANNIVERSARY

I can almost hear the wedding bells
Ringing softly in my heart
As I close my eyes and remember
How our love first got its start.

The years have gathered one by one.
Time has quietly slipped away
Leaving precious, tender memories
Of our happy wedding day.

Our Golden Anniversary
Is a dream beyond compare
That will live forever in our hearts
With the love that we both share.

We gave our love, one to the other
To keep through all the years.
And with God's help and faith
Tomorrow will hold no fear.

GOLDEN ANNIVERSARY

Wedding anniversaries are a celebration
Of that very special day,
With family and friends rejoicing
In the love God sent your way.

There are romantic memories of promise,
And marriage vows once made
That will endure forever
And never, ever fade.

Our love and years of sharing
Give life a special glow.
God has given us all of this,
More than we dreamed we'd know.

The years take their toll
As proudly they are worn.
But the ties that bind us together
Will never, ever be torn.

GOLDEN ANNIVERSARY

TO MY BELOVED WIFE
If all the treasures in the world
Were placed in one display,
I would trade them all
To be with you each day.

You are everything I've longed for,
My paradise come true.
I couldn't ask more of life
Than to spend each day with you.

TO MY LOVING HUSBAND
If all the words locked in my heart
Were suddenly set free,
They could never say
How much you mean to me.

You are my life
And have given me
A world I thought
Could never be.

As we celebrate our Golden Anniversary,
Fifty-years was only yesterday.
Thank you Lord, for all of them.
We are still in love today.

CHRISTMAS EVE
WEDDING ANNIVERSARY

Wedding bells ring on Christmas Eve
For a boy and girl in love,
United as husband and wife
In the presence of God above.

We gave our hearts to each other
To keep through all the years,
A Christmas gift to cherish
Through happiness and tears.

Christmas Eve in all its glory
Will forever and ever be
A day God made in Heaven,
And our cherished memory.

Happy Anniversary, my darling,
Our Christmas is every day.
I couldn't ask for more
Than the love God sent our way.

GOLDEN WEDDING ANNIVERSARY
AND PRICELESS MEMORIES

TO MY LOVING WIFE:

This is our wedding day.
Fifty wonderful years ago
A bit of Heaven came my way.
What a day this is going to be.
I remember the moment
That God gave you to me.
He was present - - the honored guest,
As we made our wedding vows
And then were blessed.
Golden moments, priceless in their worth,
Are my treasure of loving memories.
You are my heaven on earth.

TO MY FAITHFUL HUSBAND:

Hand in hand we made our wedding vows
And promised to be true.
What a wondrous love, then and now.
The storms of life at times were severe,
But I have never been afraid
Because you, my love, were near.
The gems of love you have given to me
I will cherish my whole life through.
They are my treasure of memories.
I will love you forever and a day.
This is my promise true.
Fifty years seem like only yesterday.

The past is a treasure of love
for a husband and wife to share.
Life's riches are within each other
a wealth beyond compare.

ANNIVERSARY LOVE

TO MY PRECIOUS WIFE: FIFTY YEARS
SEEM LIKE ONLY YESTERDAY

I LOVE YOU MY DARLING
AS I NEVER DID BEFORE
AND EVERY DAY OF EVERY YEAR
I WILL LOVE YOU EVEN MORE.

A LOOK, A TOUCH REPLACES WORDS
WE SOMETIMES FORGET TO SAY,
BUT ALWAYS HAND IN HAND
WE HAVE NEVER LOST OUR WAY.

TO MY LOVING HUSBAND: WHERE HAVE THEY
GONE…THOSE WONDER YEARS?

THE LUSTRE OF OUR MARRIAGE
ADDS BEAUTY TO THE LOVE
WE GAVE TO ONE ANOTHER
IN THE PRESENCE OF GOD ABOVE.

IN THE QUIET HOURS OF EACH DAY
WHEN WE ARE ALONE,
AND HOLDING EACH OTHER CLOSE
WE HAVE A LOVE ALL OUR OWN.

SECTION SEVEN:
HOLIDAYS

1. EASTER
2. HALLOWEEN
3. THANKSGIVING
4. CHRISTMAS

GOD'S LOVE

The pain and suffering of our Lord, Jesus,
On the cross and the agony of God at
The crucifixion of His only Son for
The salvation of the world can never
Be forgotten. The sacrifice of God,
The Father, and God, the Son, will live
Forever in the hearts of all obedient
To His commands.

God gave His only son to lead us home
To that distant shore where there is
No earthly pain or sorrow; a paradise
Of peace and love with Jesus beside you.
What greater glory could there be than
To see the face of God and live with
Him for all eternity?

In the eyes of God, all His children
Are created equal and He loves each
One...bestowing upon them the joy and
Happiness of His earthly creations.

Of all God's bounties and heavenly
Grace, there is none more joyful than
Love. For this we should be forever
Thankful and seek His way to eternal life
And a love we have never known.

JESUS, OUR SAVIOR, LIVES
FRIDAY

Come walk with me and know my love.
I make this journey for you.
I need your participation
For all that I must do.

The crown of thorns around my head
Reminds me why I'm here.
Each drop of blood a prayer
That I will have you near.

The cross I bear will hold my body
Before this task is done.
Our Heavenly Father forgives you
With this sacrifice of me, His son.

As we share these final moments
Waiting for God to take me home,
I know my journey was not in vain
For I am not alone.

Come, walk with me and know my love.
Follow me back home.
Thank our Father for His grace
And for your sins atone.

JESUS, OUR SAVIOUR, LIVES
ASCENSION

The sky was never more beautiful,
With white clouds against the blue...
A panorama of serenity
Hiding the glory of Heaven from view.

As Jesus ascended into Heaven
So shall he come again.
Midst joyous angels singing praise
For all who believe in him.

The mortal body of Christ is gone,
But we shall never part,
For his Holy Spirit lives with us...
Forever in our heart.

JESUS, OUR SAVIOR, LIVES
FOREVER

So long as there is a God in Heaven
And life in our universe,
So shall the spirit of Jesus live
In his Father's home and on earth.

The crucifixion of our Lord
Could never destroy God's power.
That plan was His to carry out.
God brought him to that hour.

The skies and earth rebelled that day
As our Savior was taken away.
Though soldiers laughed and people cried.
His Spirit is with us each day.

THE CROSS
SYMBOL OF FORGIVING LOVE

"It is finished", He cried
As His suffering set Him free.
The Crucifixion of Jesus was over
With His death on Calvary.
The cross that held His body
To Christians will always be
A symbol of forgiving love
For all the world to see.
Return Our Heavenly Father's love
That gave His only Son
To be crucified on Calvary
So that Heaven may be won.
Jesus Christ, our Savior and King,
Born to suffer for our sins,
Needs to know we're sorry
As we seek forgiveness from Him.
Tell him that you love Him
As you live your life each day.
He brought love and hope
To a world that lost its way.
Walk with the Holy Spirit
On paths that Jesus trod
As He sought to lead lost souls
Into the House of God.
The light of happiness and love
Will guide you on your way.
Our Savior did not die.
He is with you every day.

A DAY OF SORROW

In the Judgment-Hall of Pilate
Jesus was sentenced to die
And handed over to the soldiers
For them to crucify.
Bearing His cross of death
He went forth to Calvary -
Beaten and mocked along the way
For all the crowds to see.
The ridicule of soldiers
As they reveled in the pain
Of Jesus as He fell
Will forever echo in shame.
The crown of piercing thorns
Placed upon His holy head
He bore with love
For those who wished Him dead.
It was a day of sorrow.
Death help open Heaven's Door
As God took Jesus home
To reign with Him forevermore.
God gave His only son
To teach His holy creed.
Be obedient to our Father.
He will hear your every need.
The crucifixion of Jesus
Did not take Him away.
His love is now and forever.
He is with you everyday.
Humble thyself in prayer,
Seek forgiveness of your sin
And He will grant eternal life
In Paradise with Him.

THE CRUCIFIXION (1)

Crucify Him! Crucify Him!
The crowd chanted relentlessly.
Those who feared His power had spoken,
He was to die on Calvary.

They placed a crown of thorns
Upon His holy head,
Then to His heavy cross
Our Savior Christ was led.

The death march to Calvary
Was a slow and tortuous one.
Jesus was mocked and beaten
For God's teaching He had done.

From the crushing burden of His cross
He was at last set free,
Then crucified upon it
To die and live for all eternity.

THE CRUCIFIXION (2)

At daybreak in the judgment hall of Pilate
Jesus stood before him accused,
As elders of the people and high priests
Shouted their hatred and abuse.

Pilate, wishing to release Jesus, said to them,
"I find no guilt in this man",
But they cried, "Crucify him, crucify him!"
And so his destiny began.

Pilate answered, "I am innocent of his blood"
And before them washed his hands.
The people cried, "His blood be upon us forever"
And he surrendered to their demands.

THE CRUCIFIXION (2) (continued)

They led our loving Savior away
To bear his cross and thereon die,
Humbling himself to death by crucifixion
For the sins of you and I.

He carried our wrongs in silence
And was beaten and mocked for our sins.
Like sheep we have gone astray
And through his suffering are healed by him.

Each drop of blood from the crown of thorns
Placed upon his holy head
Was a prayer of forgiveness
For those who wished him dead.

Mary, Mother of Jesus, was grief stricken
As she saw him suffer for our sins.
Her sorrow had no equal -
With no comfort and no friends.

Alone in death's anguish
As Jesus was led away,
The cross was laid upon Simon of Cyrene
To help Jesus on his way.

At last they came to Golgotha,
Stripped Jesus of his clothes
And nailed him to the cross,
Rejoicing with every blow.

They placed him between two robbers
And the scripture was fulfilled.
His side and heart were pierced...
He died according to God's will.

NO GREATER LOVE

The pain and suffering of crucifixion
Flowed through his body and limbs
As he hung upon the cross
Our sins had brought to Him.

The crown of thorns
Placed upon His holy head
He wore in agony
Forgiving those who wished Him dead.

The shaft that pierced His side
Was one more act of pain
Our Savior did endure
Before His Father came.

God ended His son's sacrifice
And lovingly carried Him home.
The pain and suffering for our sins
Our Savior bore alone.

His Father surely felt His pain
For Father and Son are one.
No greater love could ever be.
God gave His only Son.

Jesus did not die on Calvary.
He lives, He lives to reign
Beside His Father in Heaven
And guide us home again.

FOR ALL WHO BELIEVE

Jesus, our Savior, the Son of God,
Was born like you and me.
Not a part of imagination
But someone we could see.

He lived, our Savior lived,
Teaching His holy words,
The unseen Spirit of God -
With words no one had heard.

He taught salvation and eternal life
For all who would follow Him
Into the Kingdom of Heaven
Free at last from mortal sin.

And then one day, His mission done,
Our Father called Him home.
He was crucified to show
That He was not alone.

For all who believe in Him
His death was not in vain.
Practice your faith in God
And love His holy name.

GOD THE FATHER

God sent his son into a world
That had forsaken Him,
To teach all people Christian love
With eternal life for them.

Jesus Christ, our Savior,
On Calvary was crucified.
He preached the word of God
And for that was sent to die.

Our Holy Father embraced
His suffering, faithful Son.
The mortal life of Christ had passed,
His earthly course now run.

Cradled in God's arms
Their Spirits joined as one,
Jesus ascended into Heaven,
His Father's will was done.

Eternal life in Heaven
Awaits those who choose to be
A disciple of God's teaching
For all the world to see.

JESUS CHRIST, SON OF GOD

His destiny was to die
In atonement for our sins.
God sacrificed His only Son
To bring us close to Him

A greater love than this
The world will never know.
The Son of God was crucified
To help His teaching grow.

He is our salvation
The Savior of our soul,
Teaching us to live with God
And Heaven as our goal.

Eternal life awaits all those
Who walk with Him
And share the burden of His cross
To free themselves from sin.

God the Father, Son and Holy Spirit
Are the Sacred Trinity
That lead us back to Him
For all eternity.

JESUS CHRIST OUR SAVIOR

Have faith in our Lord Jesus
He is to everyone a friend.
His life is now and forever
In a world that never ends.

Jesus died for each of us
That we might live again.
He needs our love to know
His death was not in vain.

Show our Lord you love Him
Open your heart with prayer.
Remember His death on Calvary
And the cross He had to bear.

Believe in His resurrection
And freedom from the grave
And you will gain eternal life
With all he died to save.

LISTEN TO JESUS

Jesus Christ, Son of God
On Calvary was crucified.
He was taken from our midst
And yet He did not die.

Our Heavenly Father joined His Son
To free Him from suffering pain
And took Him home to Heaven
Where together they will reign.

As Jesus ascended in to Heaven
His body and spirit were one
And so He shall return someday
To judge what we have done.

How will you greet Him?
What words will you say?
Take His hand and listen,
He will help you find your way.

OUR SAVIOR

Jesus needed friends,
More than he had,
And yet he gave his life for all of us,
The good, and yes, the bad.

I would have helped him had I been there,
When the burden of his cross was too much to bear.
My heart aches when I think of his pain,
And I wish that he was mortal again.

But not if he should suffer more,
God would not have it so.
I just want him in my life,
And to help his teachings grow.

He is our Savior
And to each of us a friend
God gave his only son,
So that life would never end.

EASTER GREETINGS
WRITTEN FOR SOMEONE SPECIAL

My name is Jesus
And I will be your friend,
Forever and a day
World without end.

I did not die on Calvary.
That was not my destiny.
I was born to live forever
And from sin to set you free.

The light in your eyes
Is your heart shining through
As you give to others the love
That I have given you.

May you know the happiness
That you deserve
For sharing the burdens
Of so many you serve.

JESUS AND THE EASTER BUNNY

I saw a rabbit in our yard
And excitedly told my Dad.
He said the Easter Bunny checks
If you're being good or bad.

You have to behave each day
And do your best in school.
The Easter Bunny is watching
So you better play it cool.

The Easter Bunny loves all kids.
My Mother said it's true.
But you must earn his love
And what he has for you.

There's colored eggs and candy
And even a toy or two
In a beautiful big basket
Especially for you.

Parents help the Easter Bunny
Just a little I suppose.
The Easter Bunny brings candy.
Mom and Dad new Sunday clothes.

You have to look your best
For Jesus on Easter Day,
Not that he would mind…
He loves you anyway.

Easter is when Jesus
Began his life anew.
God took him into Heaven
Where he watches over you.

Jesus lived on Earth
A long, long time ago.
I didn't know him then, of course,
But I do now, you know.

HALLOWEEN

Witches fly as goblins scurry
Down paths of moonlight,
And toothless pumpkins smile in glee
As they watch on Halloween night.

It's party time and "Trick or Treat",
With surprises and costumers galore.
Little groups of make-believe
Bouncing from door to door.

Running feet and laughter
With voices raised in fun,
Are special sounds of Halloween,
Enjoyed by everyone.

HALLOWEEN

The magical broom of a wicked witch
Was the midnight express to the moon,
As goblins and ghosts all disappeared
On a flight that left too soon.

The noise and laughter of make-believe
With tricks or treats for all
Is once again a part of the past
With happy thoughts of fall.

Many a story will linger
About this festive eve
As kids and grown-ups wonder why
These spirits had to leave.

Only the pumpkin knows
As his smile fades away
For he will join them every year
On this most happy day.

HARVEST OF THE HEART

We gather 'round Your table, Lord
And bow our heads to pray.
We thank You for life's blessings
You give to us each day.

Of all Thy bounties and Heavenly Grace
There's one that stands apart.
It's the love we have for others
A "Harvest of the Heart".

THANKSGIVING

The smell of Mom's home cooking
Wafts across the years
And loving thoughts turn homeward
As Thanksgiving Day draws near.

It's time to be with family
And other loved ones too,
To reminisce and talk of dreams
While you hold them close to you.

The toil of harvest is over.
And God's bounty we survey
As we gather in thanksgiving
And bow our heads to pray.

We count His blessings, one by one,
With thoughts about our worth
For Christmas Day will soon be here
When we celebrate His birth.

THANKSGIVING

We have so much to remember
And enjoy on this Thanksgiving Day
As we reap the bounties of God's love
And bow our heads to pray.

Fields and orchards once rich and full
Are now harvested and bare.
God's earth has once again brought forth
Wealth for His family to share.

We thank you Lord, for joy and peace
And for all who gather here
As we humbly accept your blessings
And know that You are near.

THANKSGIVING DAY

The toil of harvest is over
And fields and orchards are bare.
There's a special day for Thanksgiving
To gather together and share.

It's a day of celebration
That is always best at home.
What joy to be with friends and family
And not spend this day alone.

Home is where the heart is.
It can be anywhere.
The door is always open
To a treasure of loving care.

The bounties of God surround you
As you bow your head and pray.
Giving thanks to our Heavenly Father
For His blessings on this day.

HARVEST TIME

The harvest moon is full and bright
Shining through the haze,
Reflecting on frosty pumpkins
Between fields of golden maize.

The shadows of geese in flight
Flicker over "jelly rolls" of hay
While dancing ghosts of ages past
Stir thoughts of happy days.

The trees are draped with color
As the flowers fade away.
Beauty replaces beauty
In nature's autumn display.

The pungent odor of burning leaves
Reminds us fall is here,
As we reap the treasures of the season
That comes but once a year.

The bounty of the land is gathered,
Fields and orchards are bare,
As a harvest moon shines down
On thankful families in prayer.

THANKSGIVING

There's a hint of winter in the air
And the colors of fall disappear.
Harvest time is nearly over
As Thanksgiving Day draws near.

The bounties of Christ are gathered
From seeds that we have sown.
Love is the greatest of them all
For in the heart it's grown.

It's time to go back home again
To have friends and family near
And celebrate God's blessings
With those you hold so dear.

Home may be on a city street
Or in the country, still
It's where you'll find true love
In answer to God's will.

REMEMBER THE CHRIST CHILD

A new baby brings love
And a wondrous peace within.
God gave us Baby Jesus
To lead us back to Him.

His birthday is called Christmas
And on this Holy day,
Friends and family join together
To bow their heads and pray.

We rejoice on Christmas Day
With an exchange of gifts and love.
As distant angels sing His praise
His light shines from above.

The world unites for a moment
As the dove of peace flies high
In celebration of life
And a love that will never die.

Joy to all God's children.
His love is always there.
Remember the Christ Child,
A Gift beyond compare.

THE CHRIST CHILD

He is a special Boy,
The most Holy One -
The image of His Father
God's only precious Son.

He was born in a stable
Amongst the animals and hay -
Wrapped in ordinary cloth
In a manger the Christ Child lay.

Mary and Joseph watch o'er Him,
Their Holy infant Son,
And shepherds come to pray
At last God's will was done.

Wisemen traveled from far and near
To worship this King of Kings
And offered gifts of praise
As choirs of angels sing.

His guiding light in Heaven
God placed for all to see -
To lead them to their Savior
And life eternally.

Born to teach His Father's word
And lead us back to Him.
Jesus will always live
To free the world from sin.

Celebrate the birth of Christ,
God's gift on Christmas Day.
A love beyond compare
Time will never take away.

THE SPIRIT OF CHRISTMAS

Catch the Spirit of Christmas.
On this most holy day;
Jesus Christ, our Savior was born
To lead us in God's way.

Beautiful wrapping and ribbons
Dress gifts we give each other
The Christ Child poorly dressed
Came from God and a Virgin Mother.

Our sacred Father loved us so
He wanted His gift to be
A part of Him with hope
For life eternally.

Christmas eve in all its glory
And God's love on Christmas Day
The world will celebrate forever.
The birth of Christ brought Heaven our way.

CHRISTMAS DAY

It's Christmas Day
And in the morning's first light
I heard a baby cry
But there was none in sight.

I thought of Baby Jesus
And wondered if He knew
The task that lay before Him
And the things that He must do.

He brought us love -
A gift so hard to find
When you've forsaken God
And put Him out of mind.

Our Savior Jesus Christ was born
To teach the world God's word
And tell them of a paradise
Of which no one had heard.

If you should hear a baby cry
Early some Christmas morn
Remember the Christ Child
And the day that He was born.

CHRISTMAS INVITATION

You're invited to a party
And I hope that you'll attend.
Just to make it better,
Why not bring along a friend?

It's a birthday celebration
For our dear Lord above
And I ask the gift you bring
Be one of lasting love.

You won't need directions
No matter where you start.
If you will only follow
The light within your heart.

The time is twenty-five, December,
For all of those who care,
And on this special day,
I hope that you'll be there.

You're guaranteed a good time,
One you won't forget.
For when the party's over,
You'll be so glad you met.

Will you join the celebration
Of Him we cannot see?
Accept His invitation
And please---R.S.V.P.

CHRISTMAS JOY

The joyous sounds of Christmas
Are ringing all around
As throngs of happy people rejoice
In the spirit they have found.

Church bells tolling on Christmas Eve
Blend with voices as they sing
The praises of Our Savior
And the peace that faith can bring.

Light from the star of Bethlehem
Still shines in Heaven above
Leading all who seek Him
To His eternal love.

Christmas Day with all its joy
Has blessed us once again
As we celebrate the birth of Christ
With all who believe in Him.

REMEMBER GOD'S CHILDREN

With the birth of every child
We are given a gift of love.
This precious life is blessed
For it comes from God above.

Children need to know love.
Without this happy sign
Life is without promise
And the spirit will wither and die.

The words "I love you" broken by sobs
From a child seeking someone to care
Are words Our Savior spoke.
Tell them you are there.

When you think of Baby Jesus
Remember God's other children too.
Share the blessings and love
That God has given you.

Children never ask for much,
Only that you smile and say
"I will love you always"
And share life with them each day.

REMEMBER THE CHILDREN

In a cold, dark little bedroom
With only a candle for light
A small child lay praying
Clutching his thin blanket tight.

Christmas Day is coming
And he hoped that God would hear
The prayers and wishes of a child
At this special time of year.

He thought of Baby Jesus
And the manger where He lay
Then wished Him Happy Birthday
On this most holy day.

He asked our Heavenly Father
To keep Baby Jesus warm
And wished he had some clothes
That weren't all tattered and torn.

Christmas Eve is filled with hope
As Christmas Day draws near.
Two sleepy eyes slowly close
On a child's wishful tear.

When you think of Baby Jesus,
Remember God's other children too,
Help make a joyous Christmas-
Share what He's given you.

A LETTER TO SANTA

Dear Santa:

I'm kind of little
And don't write so well,
But thought that I should tell you
I think you're really swell.

I know you're very busy
And don't have a lot of time.
I just hope you've got a minute
To read this note of mine.

I've tried to be a good kid
And help my Mom and Dad.
If I've done some wrong things
I sure hope you won't be mad.

I'd like to have a puppy
To keep me company
'cause there's no one else at our house
Who's a little child like me.

There's one more favor you could do
Way up there in the sky.
When you visit Baby Jesus
Please tell Him I said "Hi"!

Signed: You Know Who

THE SPIRIT OF CHRISTMAS

With the spirit of Christmas
All 'round our house
There's a feeling of love
Because of my spouse.

She is wife, mother,
And Angel too
God's gift to cherish
The whole year through.

She has given us all
The best of her life
And will continue as "Grandma"
With everything nice.

Merry Christmas, my dear,
And may God bless you
For your love that makes
Family dreams come true.

And to "Baby Jesus"
What can I say...
Except, Thank you my Lord
For our Christmas Day.

ALONE

I dread the thought of holidays
When I am left alone,
And all my friends take off
To be with folks back home.

For I am one of those
Who has no place to go,
And pride won't let me speak,
So that anyone would know.

With tearful eye and aching heart,
I go my lonely way,
And wish I had a family
To make a special day.

SANTA CLAUS

He was a jolly old man
With a beard so full and white -
Wearing glasses on a cherry-red nose
To help him with his sight.

He wore ordinary clothes.
There was nothing that was red
And listened to the wish lists
That swirled 'round his silver head.

His stomach shook with laughter
As excited kids gathered around
For he looked exactly like Santa
Though no reindeer could be found.

Where did he come from?
How did he arrive?
For this moment he was real
And kept faith in Santa alive.

Was this visit a surprise from Santa?
With children clutching his sleeve
He disappeared into the crowd
Seen only by those who believe.

245

IT'S CHRISTMAS DAY

Putting toys together late at night
Barely finishing by dawn's early light
And then tumbling into bed only to hear:
"Mom, Dad, has Santa been here?"

Not wanting to stir from your warm nest,
And trying to steal a moment's rest,
You answer, "It's not yet Christmas Day,
Lie quiet and listen for Santa's sleigh".

This only lasts for a little while
And then you wake with a knowing smile,
As little voices say:
"Can we look at our presents now?
It's Christmas Day!!"

OUR HOLY GIFT

There's a Santa Claus at Christmas time
On the corner of every street -
A symbol of goodwill and giving
To everyone he meets.

Santa travels this world
With his reindeer and his sleigh
And sometimes gifts are lost
In the Heaven's Milky Way.

Jesus Christ, our gift from God
Was born on Christmas Day.
This Holy Child given to us
Will never lose His way.

Jesus brought peace and hope
To make our dreams come true.
He is a symbol of eternal love
For children and grown-ups, too.

On the corner of every street
And in the corners of your heart,
Jesus is waiting every day
And from you will never part.

HAPPY BIRTHDAY JESUS

I am God the Father
And I lovingly give you my Son.
He is called Jesus
And our spirits are joined as One.

He is a new life
With such a long way to go
To do what I have asked
And teach what you must know.

He shall go amongst all people
Revealing to them the Way -
To gain the Kingdom of Heaven
As they live their life each day.

Whoever shall believe in Him
Will also believe in Me
And live in Paradise
For all eternity.

Happy Birthday, Jesus, My Son
From you mother Mary and Me
For you will live forever
With the world as your family.

THE GREATEST GIFT

The world was given its greatest gift
When God gave His only Son,
No fancy wrapping, just swaddling clothes
As the Christ Child's life begun.

In the manger of a stable
Sweet Baby Jesus lay.
The Son of God was born
And it was Christmas Day.

In lowly surroundings
God gave the world His Son with love
As angels singing His praise
Came from Heaven above.

This sacred gift of our Father's love
Brings peace and happiness to all
Willing to accept His teachings
And answer His loving call.

Forgotten for a moment
Should be all earthly things
As we bow our heads in prayer
And listen to church bells ring.

There will never be more beautiful words
Than Jesus was born to say.
That is why we celebrate
His birth on Christmas Day.

THE BIRTH OF HOPE

In the little town of Bethlehem
With no room to spend the night
Joseph and Mary went to a stable
To rest quietly out of sight.

Mary was with child
And the birth of Jesus was near.
The time came to have her baby
And the Christ Child was born here.

The sound of cattle and sheep
Blend with a newborn baby's cries
In a manger of a stable
Where Baby Jesus lies.

The "Star of Wonder" shone brightly
In the evening sky above
Guiding all who would believe
To our Heavenly Father's love.

Shepherds summoned by angels
Followed this wondrous star
To worship with wisemen bearing gifts
Who had journeyed from afar.

The lamp held by Joseph
Will forever a symbol be
Of "The Light of the World"
For everyone to see.

Rejoice in mind and heart
The birth of our Lord.
God entered our world as Jesus
To teach His Holy Word.

Born to bring peace and hope
Through our faith in Him
By the power of the Holy Spirit
Hope will grow for freedom from sin.

By our baptism in His holy name
Just as Christ was raised by God
So also might we live a new life,
And someday be where angels trod.

KING OF KINGS

Wisemen seeking a king
Followed a shining star
God placed in heaven
To guide them from afar.
Beneath this star in Bethlehem
A new born baby lay
In the manger of a stable-
The only place to stay.
Expecting to find a King
Seated upon a throne
They found the Christ Child sleeping
With nothing of His own.
They sought a King of Nations
And found the King of Heaven instead
Born to teach God's word
To all who would be led.
Falling onto their knees
They worship their new-born King
Offering gold, frankincense and myrrh
As choirs of angels sing.
Shepherds came from far and near
Led by His star above
To praise this King of Kings
And receive His blessing and love.
His guiding light still shines
And on this holy day.
Lift your heart towards Heaven-
He will help you find your way.

SECTION **EIGHT:**
ADDITIONAL
DECLARATIONS

ALLEGIANCE

Be proud of your country and its name.
Stand tall and you will see
From ocean to ocean and mountain to plain
An AMERICAN FAMILY.

So much is owed to those who died
To make this dream come true.
Each life a thread in our flag of pride
May it always wave for you.

With the enemy met, their blood was let
Earth and water turned red.
As they gave their lives to war's terrible strife
And joined the ranks of the dead.

Muted bugles and booming guns
Blend with loving prayers.
Honor them all, dear Lord,
When duty called, our FAMILY was there.

STRIKE THREE

He couldn't believe the call
When the umpire said "Strike three!"
And throwing his bat upon home plate
He fell onto his knees.

The bouncing bat became alive
As it flew into the air
Striking the umpire on the foot
And ending - - you know where.

The umpire doubled over
But to pain he would not yield,
And swinging that fateful bat
Chased the batter 'round the field.

The roaring crowd gave wings
To the batter's flying feet
As he ran the bases with a speed
No one would ever beat.

Crossing home plate to a rousing cheer
He waved proudly to the fans
Knowing he had run the best
That he had ever ran.

The batter's prayers were answered
And the next call made his day
As the umpire went down swinging
And was ejected from the play.

THE COFFEE CUP
AND
CELL PHONE DRIVER

You must have something to drink
Every moment of every day
And a cell phone to talk on.
There's so much you have to say.

You could die of thirst,
Though no desert is around,
You need the liquid to swallow
All the words that you have found.

Take a sip and call another number.
Who knows what you may find?
There has to be something
That surely slipped your mind!

A coffee cup, a cell phone-
As you drive merrily on your way,
Ignoring everything around you
Could suddenly end your day!

Drink your coffee at home
And make your phone calls there.
Don't do it speeding in your car,
The road's for us to SAFELY share.

THE CHALLENGER SEVEN

Space shuttle Challenger stood ready
Against a sky of blue
Waiting to be boarded
By the Seven who were its crew.

One by one they bravely entered
To take their special place
And journey to horizons
Found only in outer space.

To soar above the earth
And explore the heavenly scene -
To reach for the stars and beyond,
This is the astronaut's dream.

The Challenger streaked toward Heaven
With hellish flame and sound,
Free at last from the world
To which it had been bound.

Then a shooting star broke free
From the shuttle's fiery trail
And in it carried the Challenger crew
On a flight that could not fail.

For God had chosen these astronauts
To explore His heavenly scene
Where they will soar forever
And touch their earthly dream.

As we raise our eyes toward Heaven
Where only angels trod,
The shooting stars we see
Are our astronauts with God.

In memory of the Challenger Seven, January 28, 1986: Francis "Dick"
Scobee, 46; Michael Smith, 40' Judith Resnick, 36; Ellison Onizuka, 39;
Ronald McNair, 35; Gregory Jarvis, 41; and, Christa McAuliffe, 37.